"Then **Vince** Said to **Herschel...**"

The Best Georgia Bulldog Stories Ever Told

Patrick Garbin

TRIUMPH
BOOKS

Library of Congress Cataloging-in-Publication Data

Garbin, Patrick, 1975–
Then Vince said to Herschel—: the best Georgia Bulldog stories ever told / Patrick Garbin.
    p. cm.
  Includes bibliographical references.
  ISBN-13: 978-1-60078-011-0 (alk. paper)
  ISBN-10: 1-60078-011-3 (alk. paper)
1. University of Georgia—Football—History. 2. Georgia Bulldogs (Football team)—History I. Title.
  GV958.G44G37 2007
  796.332'630975818—dc22

                                                    2007012892

This book is available in quantity at special discounts for your group or organization. For further information, contact:

Triumph Books
542 South Dearborn Street
Suite 750
Chicago, Illinois 60605
(312) 939-3330
Fax (312) 663-3557

Printed in U.S.A.
ISBN: 978-1-60078-011-0
Design by Patricia Frey
Photos courtesy of AP/Wide World Photos unless otherwise indicated.

For my wife, who supported and believed in me when many others doubted my dream of becoming a published author.

For my father, a University of Georgia football fan and professor since 1968, who taught me the essentials of writing and to pursue Georgia football and life in general with passion.

table of
contents

acknowledgments

In 1981, at the age of six, I began attending Georgia football games and instantly developed a passion for college football in general, and Georgia football, in particular. Consequently, the writing of this book is in part a culmination of the great interest I have had in Georgia football for more than a quarter-century. However, it takes considerably more than just interest to write a book. Although only my name is identified as the author of this book, numerous individuals played key roles in making it possible for "*Then Vince Said to Herschel...*" to become a reality.

First and foremost, I extend my heartfelt appreciation to my wife. As I was researching for this book, I was also completing my initial book on Georgia football and working at a full-time job at the same time. I had very little time to devote to my wife, who was pregnant; however, she continued to be generous in her devotion, support, and encouragement. Throughout my life, my parents have been pillars of strength in their efforts to facilitate the realization of any and all of my worthwhile goals. I am grateful for their support, encouragement, and assistance.

I cannot express enough appreciation to Vince Dooley and Larry Munson for writing forewords to this book. They are two of the very best in their respected fields and two of Georgia football's greatest legends. For them to take the time from very busy schedules to write forewords for a book by an unfamiliar author speaks volumes as to the kind of individuals they are.

If it were not for the assistance I received from Claude Felton and the University of Georgia's Sports Communication office, my access to Georgia football files, statistics, and contacts would have been extremely difficult to obtain. Claude Felton has been recognized as one of the best in sports information for collegiate athletics. I would like to add that he is also one of the most hospitable and cooperative people you could meet.

I am indebted to many sportswriters because their contributions on Georgia football greatly informed the present work. Morgan Blake, Ralph McGill, Jack Troy, John Stegeman, Ed Danforth, Jesse

Outlar, Furman Bisher, Bill Cromartie, and Loran Smith are a sampling of the gifted writers I wish to acknowledge. Nearly every quote found on the pages of this book was cited from the books and newspaper accounts written by these talented and distinguished writers.

This book would have been nearly inconceivable if it were not for the archival issues of *The Atlanta Constitution*, *The Atlanta Journal*, *Athens Banner-Herald*, as well as other Georgia newspapers, all of which were available on microfilm at the University of Georgia Main Library. It is at the library that I spent countless hours researching and finding the majority of the sources used in completing this project.

Finally, I am thankful for the University of Georgia football's long and storied history and tradition. Georgia is arguably one of the top 10 college football programs of all time. If not for Georgia's 115 accomplished years of play on the gridiron, far fewer stories would have been worthy of sharing than are written in the following book.

foreword

To the *real* fans:

It always amazes me when somebody decides to go digging through the long-ago history of some team. They always come up with things I'd never envision. This book is going to reach you the same way it did me. All sorts of things that happened many years ago let us all know that Georgia fans have always been the same: extremely passionate and out of their minds when it comes to beating the main part of their schedule each year.

As I write this, the United States of America had just wrapped up the greatest bowl season in the history of American football. Never have so many favored teams gotten so far behind so quickly, game after game, and yet they managed to come back in the second half and win. And if you really do remember some of the offenses that the Dogs were running back in the 1920s and '30s, then you must have been in a state of shock when you saw all those bowl games we just watched. There were things in those games that smacked of long-ago days in football: funny looking formations and people trying to hide the ball. All those great bowl games we had this winter had to bring smiles to all the old-timers. This is the case even for those guys who have been in the ground now for close to 70 years! How can we possibly match what just happened?

Was Georgia's rally against Virginia Tech one of the greatest games in the school's history? Was the Oklahoma–Boise State bowl game just like something that we all played out in the streets many years ago when we were so young and green?

Settle back to read these words now and see if some of it sticks in your memory bank. Some of these games go way, way back, and some of the plays described are just like those goofy plays we saw this past winter in the bowl games. Despite all of television's efforts, the games actually are better than they've always been. And beyond a shadow of a doubt, the girls are much better looking!

Sincerely yours,
Larry Munson
(a very old football announcer)

foreword

When I arrived at the University of Georgia in December 1963, I was fortunate to be named the head coach of a college football program already characterized by more than 70 years of rich tradition and many years of success. With Georgia's accomplished past, I learned a multitude of unforgettable stories and events that shaped its history, many of which are featured in Patrick's book.

Although a handful of college teams claim to be associated with football's first forward pass, it is generally presumed that the initial forward pass was executed when Georgia and North Carolina met at Atlanta's Athletic Park in 1895, Georgia's fourth season of football. Pop Warner and the Red and Black were so enraged with North Carolina's "fluke" pass play, Georgia challenged the opposition to a second meeting only five days later.

In 1908 against Mercer at Macon, Georgia's quarterback, George "Kid" Woodruff, was attacked during the game by not only a Mercer enthusiast but also the fan's pet bulldog. Woodruff became Georgia's head coach 15 years later; the practice fields behind the Butts-Mehre building are named in his honor. In 1920, en route to an S.I.A.A. championship, Georgia defeated Alabama 21–14 on touchdowns scored by a fumble recovery, a blocked punt, and a last-minute blocked field goal return of more than 80 yards. Nearly 80 years ago in the first game at Sanford Stadium, the Bulldogs conquered Yale 15–0 as Vernon "Catfish" Smith was responsible for every point scored in the contest.

The early days of Georgia football are also recognized by the play of Frank Sinkwich, Charley Trippi, and John Rauch. Rauch became homesick during his freshman year of 1945 and actually attempted to leave the university to return to his home state of Pennsylvania. If not for a Georgia coach spotting Rauch, suitcase in hand, about to depart from Athens, the star quarterback's career as a Bulldog may have never developed.

In 1959 I witnessed one of the greatest moments in Georgia football history when Fran Tarkenton completed a game-winning, 13-yard touchdown to Bill Herron on fourth down with just 30 seconds remaining. At the time I was an assistant coach at Auburn, the losing team, and I watched as Georgia celebrated and Sanford Stadium seemed to rock and sway and almost fall to the ground.

I can readily recall numerous memorable stories and incidents during my 25 years as head coach at Georgia. In particular, the flea-flicker and winning two-point conversion we executed to upset national champions Alabama in 1965 stands out, as well as the great upset win over mighty Rose Bowl–winner Michigan in Ann Arbor that same year. During my first five years, our teams won two SEC championships with great players, such as All-Americans Bill Stanfill and Jake Scott, as well as Billy Payne, the best 60 minute player I ever coached. Payne later gained national distinction for bringing the 1996 Centennial Olympics to Atlanta and is now chair of the Masters golf tournament in Augusta, Georgia. Most notably, my 17th team at Georgia, the undefeated 1980 Bulldogs, were declared the University of Georgia's first undisputed national champion. Thousands of Bulldog followers and I will not soon forget freshman sensation Herschel Walker, who ran past and through the opposition, including Notre Dame in the Sugar Bowl. During those years (1980–1983) our teams won three SEC championships, a national championship, and had a record of 43–4–1. Lastly, one of my fonder memories was capturing my 200th career win over Georgia Tech in my final season of 1988. After the victory, I was joined by my family on the field, including my wife Barbara, for the first time in 25 seasons as a head coach. She proudly carried with her our first grandson, Patrick Dooley Cook.

Since my retirement as Georgia football's head coach nearly two decades ago, the Bulldogs have continued to enjoy a successful and winning tradition. In 1992 Georgia experienced an absolutely improbable triumph when time ran out on Auburn as it attempted to line up and run a play for a would-be winning touchdown on the Bulldogs' goal line. In 1997, led by Mike Bobo and Robert Edwards, Georgia stunned Florida 37–17 as the Gators' seven-game winning streak over the Bulldogs was halted. Three years later, in similar fashion, Tennessee's long winning streak over Georgia was stopped at nine games.

One of the wisest decisions I made during my tenure as athletics director was to hire Mark Richt as head football coach. Since Coach Richt's arrival in 2001, the Bulldogs are currently enjoying one of the most successful periods in Georgia football history. During the four seasons from 2002 to 2005, Georgia made three trips to the SEC championship game, winning two SEC titles in the process. The latest season of 2006 witnessed a team that by mid-November had been forgotten by many, only to have the Bulldogs finish the season with three unlikely and impressive victories.

The aforementioned events and anecdotes concerning Georgia football are only a handful of the approximately 120 stories in this book. Patrick Garbin, a historian of college football and Georgia football, covers the university's entire 115-year storied history, from its first win over Mercer in 1892 to the comeback victory over Virginia Tech in the 2006 Chick-fil-A Bowl. His countless hours of research and writing on this subject, on which he is an absolute expert, have produced this one-of-a-kind book.

There are so many extraordinary events and stories from the rich history and tradition of Georgia football, many of which are described on the following pages. I am certainly proud that for 40 years as Georgia's head coach or athletic director, I was a part of many of them.

—Vince Dooley

chapter 1

The Opening Kickoff

The brilliant and dynamic Dr. Charles Holmes Herty poses in 1930, some 40 years after bringing the game of football to the University of Georgia.

"Rah, Rah, Rah, Ta Georgia"

Twenty-two years following football's first intercollegiate game between Princeton and Rutgers, Dr. Charles Herty of the University of Georgia began assembling one of the first college football teams in the Southeast. In the fall of 1891 there was no opposition for Herty's Georgia squad, as no other institutions in the general area had a team. However, Mercer College agreed to field a football squad and face Georgia sometime after Christmas.

On January 30, 1892, the Deep South's first college football game was played between Georgia and Mercer on a playing field situated immediately behind Georgia's New College. Georgia's starting 11 averaged 5'10" inches in height and 157 pounds in weight—scant compared to college football's current standards. Just before the 3:00 PM start, many of the 1,500 in attendance hollered for the home team, "Rah, rah, rah, ta Georgia!" The cheer may have been similar to the current tradition of "calling the dogs," exhibited by Georgia fans. Instead, it may have been the crowd's way of "calling the goats," as a goat, not a bulldog, was Georgia's first mascot in 1892.

On the first play of the first game played in Georgia football history, Mercer, considered "no slouch," lost three yards from scrimmage. Georgia's first score and touchdown soon followed when captain Frank Herty, nephew of Coach Charles Herty, touched down behind the Mercer goal for four points on an "extraordinary" run. A touchdown counted for four points until 1898, when the point value increased to five.

Halfback Herty scored five and a half touchdowns against Mercer—a would-be school record to this day if insufficient documentation did not prevent most statistics prior to the 1940s from being considered official. Herty is credited with half a touchdown—he and fullback Henry Brown somehow scored Georgia's last touchdown together; the manner by which this was accomplished was not reported. Brown also made four kicks after touchdowns, which counted for two points each. Other Georgia scoring included three touchdowns by halfback John Kimball and a touchdown and safety (two points) by guard George Shackelford.

The *Atlanta Constitution* reported that spectators' hats were tossed into the air after the game and Georgia players were hoisted onto the shoulders of patrons in celebration as "the red and crimson of the University of Georgia waves triumphantly, and a score of 50 to nothing shows the university boys know how to play football." Reportedly, the final score should have been 60–0, but the official scorer made two trips to the Broad Street dispensary during the game and missed two touchdowns and a successful kick after a touchdown by Georgia.

Three weeks later, the Deep South's oldest rivalry began when Georgia and Auburn played in Atlanta's Piedmont Park. Auburn won 10–0 and ended Georgia's inaugural season with a 1–1 record. It would be the first of only 35 campaigns in 113 seasons of Georgia football through 2006 that Georgia had a nonwinning season.

Darkness Defeats "Alabamians"

After losing to Auburn, or the "Alabamians," in 1892, Georgia did not play them the following season. In fact, 1893 is just one of five seasons from 1892 to the present when the two rivals did not play one another. In 1917 and 1918 Georgia did not field a team because of World War I, while Auburn canceled its 1943 season because of World War II. The two schools would have played in 1897, except that Georgia called off its remaining schedule after tragically having a player die from an injury incurred in a game against Virginia on October 30.

On November 24, 1894, at Atlanta's Athletic Park, Georgia played Auburn for the second time. Georgia entered the game, having won three consecutive contests by a combined score of 116–0 under the guidance of Robert Winston—the school's first paid football coach. At the time, neither schools had the nickname it has today; it would be several years had known as the "Georgia Bulldogs" and "Auburn Tigers." Ironically, the *Athens Banner* declared that "the Georgians played like tigers."

The game was extremely exciting and fiercely played before the largest crowd ever to witness a football game in Atlanta. As darkness fell, both teams' uniforms were so soiled it was difficult to distinguish between the two squads. Georgia's Herb Stubbs scored his second touchdown as Georgia went ahead, only to see Auburn quickly knot the score at 8–8.

Late in the game, with Auburn backed up near its goal line, the Alabamians asked for the game to be called because of darkness and for the game to end in a tie. Georgia refused Auburn's request. While attempting to punt behind his goal line, Auburn's fullback lost the snap in the shadows. Trying to pick up the dropped snap, the fullback was tackled behind the line for a safety by Georgia's center Rufus Nalley and guard Fred Price. Now Georgia requested that the game be called, but this time Auburn refused. Nevertheless, Georgia held onto its 10–8 lead and improved its record to 4–1. That evening a fairly large number of Athenians and university students met the victors returning from Atlanta with a brass band and a nighttime torchlight procession.

The Inception of the Forward Pass

There has been some debate regarding which teams and individuals were involved in the first forward pass in college football history. Some feel that Walter Camp of Yale threw the first legal forward pass to Oliver Thompson for a touchdown against Princeton in 1891. However, it is generally believed that the initial forward pass actually occurred in Georgia's game versus North Carolina on October 26, 1895. The first forward pass was executed September 5, 1906, when Saint Louis University's Bradbury Robinson passed to teammate Jack Schneider.

Georgia had a successful 5–1 season in 1894. The following year, coached by the eventual, immortal Glenn "Pop" Warner, it was revealed by the *Constitution* before the season that "the improvement of the present Georgia team over the last season's team is almost too much to comprehend." Georgia began its 1895

Legend has it that Glenn "Pop" Warner's 1895 team, which hadn't lost a game in nearly a year, succumbed to the first forward pass, albeit an illegal one, in a 6–0 loss to North Carolina.

campaign by walloping Wofford College 34–0, and a week later faced North Carolina, which was acknowledged as a football powerhouse and the South's second-best team behind Virginia.

Inconceivably, some of the "vast crowd" of 1,000 spectators at Atlanta's Athletic Park stood on the field behind the offensive team during the game, unwilling to remain on the sidelines. Early in the scoreless contest, North Carolina's punter retreated with the ball but was hemmed in between Georgia's oncoming defenders and the fans who were on the field behind the offense. In desperation, the Tar Heel punter illegally threw downfield to a startled teammate, who caught the ball and ran 70 yards for a touchdown.

The referee allowed the play, alleging he did not see the forward pass. Georgia followers were livid, including Pop Warner, who protested to the referee to no avail. The Tar Heels took a 6–0 lead that they would not relinquish and handed Georgia its first defeat in nearly a year. The next day, the *Constitution* called North Carolina's scoring pass "clearly a fluke," and said "on the merits of actual play, the score should have stood 0 to 0."

Greatly irritated over the "fluke" play, the Georgians challenged North Carolina to return to Atlanta five days later, on Halloween, to face them for a second time. The Tar Heels obliged and defeated Georgia 10–6 in a cold rain in front of only 350 spectators at Athletic Park. North Carolina's return trip was the first of only four times through 2006 when Georgia faced the same opponent two or more times in the same season.

More so than when the first forward pass was thrown, there may be more disagreement as to who threw and caught the first forward pass. The *Journal* reported that North Carolina's George Stephens passed to Joel Whitaker, while Auburn coach John Heisman, who was at the game scouting Georgia, claimed that Stephens was on receiving end, not the passer.

In 1905 Heisman formally requested of the proper collegiate football authorities to make the forward pass part of the college game in order to open up the sport and make it more exciting. A year later the forward pass was allowed by the game's rules.

Rosalind Gammon Saves Football in Georgia

In the season following its first undefeated and untied campaign of 1896, Georgia began the year by shutting out both Clemson and Georgia Tech. Much of the team's early success could be attributed to fullback Richard "Von" Gammon of Rome, Georgia— one of Georgia's best players and the quarterback of the undefeated 1896 squad.

On October 30, 1897, Georgia and Virginia played at Atlanta's Brisbine Park in a much anticipated encounter. Following a Virginia touchdown and conversion, Georgia's Brooks Clark blocked a Cavalier punt that Billy Kent recovered for a touchdown. Some odds had been set at 2-to-1 before the game that Georgia would not score against Virginia. The Cavaliers later scored a field goal and led 11–4 at halftime.

Early in the second half Gammon was trying to make a tackle on defense. In his attempt, he fell to the ground and was instantly toppled on top of by several players of both teams. The mass of players unpiled, except Gammon, who continued to lie on the ground in a semiconscious state. Some time went by before he was carried off of the field and taken to Grady Memorial Hospital by ambulance. The game resumed, but Georgia—having lost Gammon and another standout, quarterback Reynolds Tichenor, to injury—played with little enthusiasm. Virginia added another touchdown and eventually won 17–4.

At some point, Gammon lost consciousness that he would never regain. At 3:45 in the morning the day after the accident, Gammon, who was only 18 years old, died in the hospital from a severe brain hemorrhage.

The Georgia football team promptly cancelled its remaining schedule for 1897, and half the squad vowed they would never play football again. Soon it appeared that the game of football in Georgia would be prohibited by an act of the state legislature. Three days following the incident, the *Athens Banner* declared the game "on its last legs" and "football in Georgia is a thing of the past.…There will be no more of this brutality witnessed on Georgia's soil." An antifootball bill was introduced, stating that a misdemeanor would be charged to anyone playing football in the state of Georgia "where an admission fee is charged for admission to the game."

On November 2 Dr. Charles Herty, the founder of football at Georgia, wrote that the sport should not be abolished. Instead, the state should provide a suitable gymnasium at the University of Georgia so students could be properly trained in athletics in order to avoid further fatal incidents. Soon after Herty's position was made known, Gammon's mother, Rosalind Burns Gammon, wrote to her county's representative: "Grant me the right to request that my boy's death should not be used to defeat the most cherished object of his life."

Upon reading Mrs. Gammon's wishes, the governor of Georgia refused to sign the antifootball bill. Football resumed at the University of Georgia the following season on October 8, 1898, with a 20–8 victory over Clemson.

Progression of a Border War

The University of Georgia football team has recently had problems defeating its interstate rival, Florida. Since the start of the 1990s, the Bulldogs have beaten the Gators just twice in 17 tries through the 2006 season. Prior to Florida's recent good fortune, it was rarely able to defeat its neighbors to the north, as the Bulldogs were 15–2 versus the Gators from 1931 through 1948 and 13–3 from 1974 through 1989. Georgia also won the first seven games played in the series, outscoring Florida 244–9, including six shutouts.

In its first football season of 1904, Florida was, in a word, miserable. Prior to facing Georgia that year, it had lost its first two games by a combined 73–0 score. That season, Georgia's head coach was Charles Barnard—an All-American player at Harvard just three years prior. Barnard's top assistant, M.M. Dickinson, had held the head position at Georgia in 1903.

At the beginning of the 1904 season, scoring values changed again. A drop kick or field goal was worth four points instead of the previous five, touchdowns remained valued at five points apiece, and point after touchdowns continued to be worth one point each. A team still had to gain just five—but hard earned—yards for a first down. This number of yards would double to 10 when forward passing was allowed in 1906.

On October 15, 1904, Georgia, which brought 18 players, and the University of Florida, also known as Florida State College of Lake City, faced off at Macon's Central City Park at 3:00 PM. According to the *Macon Telegraph*, the Central City Park field was regarded as being in as good shape as any in the entire South, but curiously "the gridiron for the most part is covered with grass—part of it is bare."

The *Telegraph* reported that "from the first to the last minute of play it was plain to the 700 spectators that the Floridians were completely at the mercy of the Athens team." Georgia's halfback Charlie Cox scored four touchdowns, but the victors were primarily led by their 120-pound quarterback, Harry Woodruff. The quick and dodgy Woodruff scored two touchdowns, including returning a kickoff nearly 100 yards for a score. In its season-opening game, Georgia pounded the dreadful Florida team 52–0.

Florida would lose its final two games to finish its inaugural season with a record of 0–5 and was outscored for the year 225–0. The Georgia win would be its lone victory of the season as it lost its final five games by an average of slightly more than 10 points per defeat. Coach Barnard would depart after the season. The team's assistant at the time and head coach in 1903, Dickinson, would return to the head coaching position in 1905.

It is hard to believe that a touchdown and a field goal were once worth the same number of points, a field that was partly bare was considered one of the South's best gridirons, and Georgia and Florida once combined to win just one of 11 games in a season. College football has certainly changed over the last 100 years.

A Game of Firsts

Toward the end of the 1906 season, Georgia was perhaps mired its worst losing period in its entire history. Prior to its game against Auburn and dating back to after the Florida victory in 1904, Georgia had a 2–13–1 record and had been shut out on 11 occasions. Auburn, on the other hand, was in the process of establishing itself as one of the premier football programs in the South. Following the 1906 season, Auburn would win 72 percent of its games and experience just one losing campaign over the next 20 seasons.

The day before Georgia's game with Auburn in 1906, Coach Mike Donahue of Auburn told a newspaper that his squad should defeat Georgia by two touchdowns. On Thanksgiving Day, the teams squared off in Macon with 3,000 fans in attendance.

Auburn threatened to score in the first half, but the Athenians defended their goal, and at halftime the contest remained scoreless. In the second half, Georgia drove into field-goal position. With Morton Hodgson holding, Dick Graves booted a field goal, and Georgia took a 4–0 lead.

Auburn threatened to score twice more before the end of the game. Halfback Hodgson ended the first threat by intercepting a pass. The Alabamians later got within a foot of Georgia's goal line. On its last down, Auburn ran the ball straight ahead but was met by Harold "War Eagle" Ketron, who dropped the runner for a yard loss. Ketron was one of Georgia's first prominent stars and was said to, on occasion, spit tobacco juice in his opponent's eye before making a tackle. More than 30 years later, Ketron was also credited with luring the great Charley Trippi to Georgia from Pittston, Pennsylvania. As a UGA football booster, Ketron offered Trippi a scholarship, an action that now is certainly, and has been so for quite some time, against NCAA regulations.

Following Ketron's game-saving tackle, Georgia held on for only its second victory of the season. The *Telegraph* proclaimed there was "great rejoicing in Macon, and Red and Black are celebrating all over town." The win over Auburn was very significant because it turned an apparently dreadful season into somewhat of a success. Morton Hodgson had made the first recorded interception in Georgia history, while Graves's successful kick was seemingly Georgia's first-ever game-winning field goal occurring in the final period of play.

chapter 2

From Controversy to Prosperity

George Woodruff, a star quarterback and later coach, once had to fend off a wild Mercer fan with his hands and the man's bulldog with his legs during a melee after a game in Macon.

No Coach, No Problem

Despite a 57–0 victory over Dahlonega to open the 1907 season, and having scored the most points by any college team on that particular day, the local media considered the 1907 Georgia team inferior to its 1905 or 1906 squads. Those two teams had a combined record of only 3 wins, 9 losses, and one tie.

During a 10–6 loss to Georgia Tech, Grantland Rice, a writer for the *Nashville Tennessean,* later wrote that Georgia coach W.S. Whitney had used at least four illegal players, including individuals who had previously played at Georgetown, Syracuse, and a professional team in Savannah. The ineligible players reportedly received $150, plus all travel expenses for their losing efforts against Georgia Tech.

Coach Whitney admitted that because of pressure from alumni following an earlier 15–0 loss to Tennessee, players were recruited to play for Georgia who had prior college or professional experience. However, according to Whitney, he was not aware that any of these players were compensated.

The Southern Intercollegiate Athletic Association (SIAA) conducted an investigation and ruled that Georgia was guilty of using the illegal players. The school was later reinstated in the association, but captain Kyle Smith was suspended for the season finale versus Auburn and assistant coach Branch Bocock was ordered to watch the game from the stands. Whitney received the harshest penalty—banishment for life from coaching in the South.

Georgia slumped into Macon's Central City Park for its annual Thanksgiving Day game against Auburn with no coach and a substitute captain, Erle Newsome. According to writer Kenneth Todd, Georgia's "eyes looked about the field for a glimpse of Coach Bocock, who succeeded Coach Whitney, but the glances were futile. There was no coach in sight." To make the situation worse, it was cold and rainy and the playing field was extremely muddy. Furthermore, the Red and Black were figured to be a huge underdog of two or more touchdowns.

During halftime, with the scoreboard surprisingly scoreless, Georgia's players availed themselves of whatever means necessary to stay warm and dry. According to an eyewitness Georgia fan, tackle Herman DeLaPerriere drank the contents of a small flask. He would then return the second-half kickoff all the way to midfield, where he was met by a trio of tacklers. DeLaPerriere required several minutes before he could re-enter the game, either because he had to recuperate from the vicious hit, or perhaps to recover from what he drank from the flask.

With roughly 14 minutes remaining in the contest, Harry Harmon of Georgia batted an Auburn pass to the ground. It was considered a free ball in the early days of the sport. Jim Lucas scooped up the rolling football and scooted 50 yards for a touchdown. Cliff Hatcher's conversion was successful, and Georgia held on to its 6–0 lead for an eventual victory.

The Auburn contest was acclaimed by some as the greatest game ever played in Macon at that time and the most significant victory by Georgia in its brief, 16-season history. The Red and Black's 4–3–1 final record was their best in five years, and they finished in third place in the 11-member SIAA. This was quite an accomplishment for a team for which pundits had low expectations and a team that finished its season without a captain or a coach.

Fumbling Rescues Georgia

Led by standout quarterback and eventual head coach George Woodruff, Georgia played its first road game of 1908 against Tennessee after beginning the season with wins over Dahlonega and South Carolina in Athens. Tennessee had been regarded as one of the better squads in the SIAA, losing just twice in its last 13 contests dating back to the beginning of the 1907 season, while surrendering a total of only 22 points.

Against a staunch Tennessee defense, Georgia threatened to score a number of times. However, the Red and Black had trouble holding on to the ball and fumbled on a couple of occasions near the Tennessee goal. Twelve minutes into the game, J. Walker Leach, a halfback and the captain of Tennessee, scored on a 30-yard run. Leach would kick the point after and later a field goal as Georgia fell in Knoxville and lost its first contest of the season 10–0.

A story by Dr. Steadman Sanford, chancellor of the University, was later told about one of Georgia's several missed scoring opportunities against Tennessee. The Red and Black had reached the host's 5-yard line and were threatening to score on Tennessee for the first time in three series games since 1903. Suddenly, a repulsive, hateful-looking man standing on the sidelines, who was full of "venom and sour-mash whisky," made a gesture toward his hip pocket. Apparently shouting at Georgia's Woodruff, the evil-eyed Tennessee fan declared, "The first so-and-so that crosses that there mark [goal line] is going to get a .38 bullet in his carcass." Promptly and perhaps purposely, Woodruff fumbled on the very next play. Tennessee recovered the ball. Tennessee would soon be forced to punt from near its own goal. "And so, for the first and only time on record, a punter kicked both his team and the opposition out of danger," inscribed writer Edwin Camp.

Sic 'Em!

A week after having been threatened to be shot in Knoxville, quarterback Woodruff and the rest of the Red and Black traveled to Central City Park of Macon, Georgia, to face Mercer. The contest is best known for what took place off the field, as the game was marred by fighting between spectators, players, and even coaches. In particular, it will be remembered for one of the most peculiar incidents in Georgia football history.

Fighting began prior to the beginning of the game, when some of the 5,000 spectators climbed over the wire fencing that surrounded the field and invaded the playing area. This led to students of Mercer and Georgia facing off in a physical confrontation. During this time, two Mercer students inexplicably gave Georgia assistant coach Tom Kirby a "good pummeling."

After peace was restored, Georgia and Mercer kicked off for the fourth time in history. The Red and Black had the ball in

Mercer's territory for most of the first half but, similarly to the week before, missed several scoring opportunities. Instead of fumbling away scoring chances, as was the case against Tennessee, Georgia's Claude Derrick missed three place kicks, or field goals, before halftime.

In the second half, Woodruff, "one of Georgia's swiftest, best players," according to the *Constitution*, and the star of the game, rallied his team to victory. Howell Peacock ran for a touchdown following a Woodruff fumble recovery, and Erle Newsome later scored for Georgia on a short plunge.

Following the victory by the Red and Black, captain DeLaPerriere of Georgia and Mercer's starting right end, Bob Poole, sought out one another—they had had a series of heated verbal exchanges during the game. In the meantime, Newsome and Mercer's Tom Farmer began to argue, and soon, according to the *Telegraph*, "it was a free-for-all fight with Mercer and Georgia players and several hundred excited spectators mixed in the melee."

During one of the many altercations, a Mercer fan and his pet bulldog dashed from the sidelines onto the field to join the fracas. The Mercer follower physically attacked Woodruff while also siccing his bulldog on the Georgia quarterback. Woodruff had to ward off a Mercer double-team, protecting his upper body from punches thrown by the fan, while trying to keep his legs from being bitten by the bulldog.

The *Telegraph* described Georgia's 11−0 victory over Mercer as "one of the most disgraceful occurrences in the history of athletics in Macon." In a game acknowledged more for its fighting than its football, Woodruff will be remembered for not only starring on the gridiron but also for his scuffle against both man and man's best friend.

The Times They Are A-Changin'

Prior to the 1910 season the Georgia football program had been mediocre at best, lacking any semblance of winning consistency during its short history. Dr. Sanford was in the process of searching for the school's 15th head coach, hopefully one who would remain at Georgia for more than one or two seasons. Eleven of the Red and Black's first 18 seasons had been non-winning campaigns, including 1909. Georgia was coming off of a 1–4–2 season, during which it scored a total of 14 points, with only three points being made in its first five games of the year.

One day during the spring of 1910, Sanford was watching the Georgia baseball team face the Gordon Military Institute of Barnesville, Georgia. Sanford admired the manner in which Gordon's coach, Alex Cunningham, managed his players in a 12–0 Gordon victory. After the game, Sanford offered Georgia's head coaching position to Cunningham, not for baseball but for football. The baseball coach indicated that he was earning $1,300 per year at Gordon. Sanford offered $1,350, Cunningham accepted and signed a contract that was written on the back of an envelope. Many years later Cunningham said, "He didn't know it, but I would have taken the job for nothing." Importantly, freshman Bob McWhorter of the Gordon Institute would be joining his coach at Georgia—he had already planned to attend the university in the fall of 1910. Cunningham would bring several other star athletes with him from Gordon to Athens, including Hafford Hay and John "Tiny" Henderson.

Despite the new additions, it was predicted that the 1910 season would be another losing year for the Red and Black. Only five players returned from the season before, while most of Georgia's heralded newcomers failed to meet entrance requirements. In addition, the team's schedule was thought to be the most difficult in its history, despite starting the season matched against two preparatory schools.

Led by McWhorter's five touchdowns, Georgia opened the season by pounding Locust Grove Institute 101–0. A week later on a slippery surface at Herty Field, Cunningham and McWhorter faced their old school. The Red and Black recorded their second consecutive substantial shutout with a 79–0 victory over Gordon. McWhorter scored seven of Georgia's 14 touchdowns. The game was called after three quarters because of the exhaustion of Gordon's players. One particular visiting player was so exhausted after chasing McWhorter during one of his seven scores that he fell to the ground and had to be carried off the field in serious condition. Because of this incident and the game result, "the authorities at the University of Georgia...abolished forever playing of prep teams by varsity," according to the *Atlanta Journal*.

Coach Cunningham remains one of Georgia's most successful head coaches, winning at least twice as many games as he lost in seven of his eight seasons. He finished with nearly a 68 percent winning percentage at a school that won just 47 of 109 games in its history prior to his arrival. Cunningham was Georgia's first coach to conduct strenuous practices, while his leadership qualities inspired his teams to continue fighting until the very end of games. Unlike prior Georgia coaches, he also had the kind of personality that was instrumental in rallying support from the alumni.

Besides Herschel Walker and possibly Frank Sinkwich and Charley Trippi, McWhorter is arguably the best player in the history of Georgia football. He was selected All-Southern Conference in all four of his seasons and was chosen Georgia's first All-American in 1913. He scored 61 career touchdowns, scoring no fewer than 12 in a season, and recorded two or more touchdowns in 19 of his 34 career games. In comparison, Walker scored two or more touchdowns in 16 of 36 collegiate games. Most importantly, McWhorter and Cunningham, nearly by themselves, transformed Georgia football from a substandard program into one of the most respected in the South.

Flying Headgear

When the Red and Black played at Sewanee on November 5, 1910, undefeated Georgia was considered a "wonder" because of its surprising success after years of mediocrity and a "perfect football machine in perfect condition," according to the *Journal*. It was the best Georgia team ever at that point in time, and in five games that season it had outscored the opposition by more than 50 points per contest.

Georgia was still an underdog to the Sewanee Purple Tigers who, along with Vanderbilt, had long ago established themselves as some of the best in the South. To make matters worse, two Sewanee players whose eligibility was protested by Georgia were given permission to play.

Midway through the final quarter, with Georgia losing 15–0, Coach Cunningham's squad displayed its fighting spirit of playing hard until the very end. McWhorter first returned a punt 80 yards for a score. Then Hay's successful conversion cut Sewanee's lead to nine points.

With approaching darkness and the presence of a heavy fog, Georgia had the ball on Sewanee's 25-yard line late in the contest. Woodruff lofted a long pass downfield. However, what was being thrown was not the football but a piece of headgear. Fooled by the Red and Black, Sewanee defenders chose to chase the lofted object, while Hay, with the actual football, ran for a touchdown.

Soon after the chicanery, the game was called because of darkness. The Purple Tigers won the game by a score of 15–12. It would be one of only six losses for the Red and Black in four seasons from 1910 to 1913. Against Sewanee, Georgia may have lost "one of the hardest-fought gridiron battles ever staged in the South" but implemented perhaps the most unusual trick play ever executed in college football.

chapter 3

Pre–WWI Pigskin Plots and Happenings

The Georgia Bulldogs marched off to World War I with the rest of America, and the football program was suspended in 1917–18.

A New Field, A New Beginning

Georgia's 21–0 victory over Mercer on October 29, 1910, was the last game played by the Red and Black on Herty Field, their initial gridiron. It can be deduced that Herty Field had a decisive home-field advantage. In 19 seasons of playing there, Georgia achieved a record of 23–14–2 (.615) compared to winning less than 44 percent of its games at other sites during the same time. Georgia's success at home included the period from the 1895 season until November 1900, when it won 10 consecutive games at Herty Field, outscoring the opposition 210–8, while holding all but one of the opponents scoreless.

Sanford Field was constructed just off of Lumpkin Street in Athens and was to be a combined football field and baseball diamond. The money for the field's construction was raised by Dr. Steadman Sanford and Hugh Gordon, a Georgia football letterman in 1900. Sanford Field would soon be considered one of the finest gridirons in the South, in part because it featured a covered grandstand.

After Georgia's unexpected success in 1910, when the Red and Black finished with a 6–2–1 record, there was a heightened interest in the squad the following season. It was anticipated that the team would be the best ever at Georgia. Most of the players returned from the year before, while several prep school stars had also enrolled. Significantly, halfback Bob McWhorter was returning after a freshman season when he was regarded by many, including *Journal* writer Pete Daley, as "without a doubt the most feared player in the South."

Georgia hosted Alabama Presbyterian for the 1911 season opener and the inaugural game at Sanford Field. After the opening kickoff, the first offensive play on the new field was a 90-yard touchdown pass from Tom Powell to McWhorter. Georgia would never look back as McWhorter scored twice more in the final quarter. Powell added two touchdowns, including one occurring on a 50-yard fumble return. The Red and Black blanked the "Preds" 51–0.

Antismoking in Athens

Georgia's 13–3–2 combined record for the 1910 and 1911 season had been unprecedented in the program's history, and the 1912 season was expected to be even more successful. Captained by right guard David "Emp" Peacock, the Red and Black's expectations of being a championship team were "authentic, speaking from the standpoint of material," according to the *Constitution*.

The optimistic outlook began to dim when six players broke training before the season-opening game against Chattanooga and were dismissed from the team for smoking. Despite the loss in personnel, Georgia defeated Chattanooga 33–0, with McWhorter scoring three touchdowns, although he only participated in two quarters.

On the Monday following the win, the university's student body met in the University Chapel to discuss the dismissed players. A petition containing a series of resolutions was signed and passed by a nearly unanimous vote. One of the resolutions pertained to the reinstatement of the dismissed players. Actually, this was the first time in a number of years that any player had been dismissed from the football squad for breaking training. It was generally felt that banishment from the team because of smoking was too severe of a punishment. The last resolution in the petition interestingly stated that "in the future any man who deliberately breaks training shall be looked upon by the students as an enemy of the Georgia spirit."

Manifesting the Georgia spirit, the team, including the reinstated smokers, defeated Citadel the following Saturday by the exact score of its opening game, 33–0. McWhorter, only playing the first quarter, caught a 60-yard touchdown pass from Timon Bowden on the second play of the game. The highlight of the contest was the running of Georgia reserve quarterback E.H. Dorsey. Dorsey weighed a scant 110 pounds but managed to rush for gains of 30 and 40 yards.

Water Boy Reception/Deception

Following Georgia's 2–0 start in 1912, the Red and Black were soundly beaten by Vanderbilt 46–0. The loss had to be extremely bitter for Coach Alex Cunningham—he was a graduate of Vanderbilt, lettering in football only four years prior to his arrival at Georgia in 1910. The 46-point loss was the Red and Black's worse since 1901; it would be nearly two decades before they endured one of a greater margin. Entering the fourth game of the season versus Alabama, Georgia's morale was at its lowest since Cunningham became head coach, and the team's spirit needed to be raised.

Cunningham concocted a plan he hoped would elevate his squad's confidence in its game against Alabama. Following is an abbreviated version of what transpired as reported in the *Constitution*: "First quarter. Alabama kicked off. Wheatley returning 15 yards. [Alonzo] Awtrey, in citizen's clothes on the sideline, caught a forward pass of Bowden's and made 35 yards." A citizen on the sideline caught a pass thrown by Georgia?

Prior to the game, Georgia's Awtrey dressed out in a pair of white overalls rather than the standard football uniform. Only 10 players lined up to receive Alabama's opening kickoff, while Georgia's 11th man, Awtrey, stood on the sideline, disguised and holding a water bucket, creating the impression that he was the water boy. After Georgia returned the opening kickoff, Awtrey casually remained on the sideline as the Red and Black lined up for its first play. When Bowden dropped back to pass, Awtrey dropped his bucket and ran downfield. Bowden completed his toss to Awtrey around midfield where the "water boy" ran for an additional 35 yards.

Bedlam broke out on the field. In protest of the trick play, Alabama fans engulfed the playing field, followed by many of Georgia's faithful, intent on protecting their team. Fights ensued between fans and players, while the police began randomly making arrests. Witnessing the chaos his trickery had caused, Cunningham suggested that the play should not count and the ball be brought back to the original line of scrimmage. The officials, however, indicated there was nothing in the rule book specifying the type of uniform a player must wear. The play stood, but Alabama recovered a McWhorter fumble on the next play. It would be the first of many fumbles lost in an unexpectedly close game.

Alabama surprisingly took a 6–0 lead in the second quarter when Everett Wilkinson blocked a Georgia punt and recovered it for a score. In the same quarter, Bowden rushed for a 30-yard touchdown, and the successful conversion gave the Red and Black a one-point lead. Georgia, a three-touchdown favorite, fell behind again following a Wilkinson field goal in the third quarter.

With five minutes remaining in the contest, Alabama reached Georgia's 15-yard line and lined up to attempt a field goal. The snap was bad and recovered by Bowden, who ran for 25 yards before being tackled. On the next play, Georgia's Charlie Thompson, filling in for an injured McWhorter, caught a touchdown pass from Bowden. The Red and Black held on to its 13–9 lead to defeat 'Bama for the third consecutive season. Besides Bowden's standout performance, John Henderson of Georgia remarkably recovered at least five fumbles.

Just Like Home

Dave Paddock of Brooklyn, New York, was not very fond of the northern winters. Following high school, he wanted to attend a reputable agricultural school in the South. A friend suggested the University of Georgia.

Paddock tried out for the 1912 football team. Although he had been captain of his high school team, it would be difficult to earn a spot on a talented Georgia squad, considered to be the best ever at the school. Paddock, however, did make the team as a halfback. Later in the season, he played on a limited basis but proved to be ineffective.

Prior to the Georgia Tech game on November 16, Coach Cunningham decided to move Paddock from halfback to quarterback. This decision was based in part on the desire to take advantage of Paddock's tremendous speed. Led by Bob McWhorter, who gained 163 yards on 31 carries and scored two touchdowns in the process, Georgia toppled the Yellow Jackets 20–0. In his first game at quarterback, Paddock was also sensational, once rushing for 57 yards from a punt formation. After the game, the young quarterback was congratulated by one of the greatest baseball players of all time, Ty Cobb.

Twelve days later, on Thanksgiving Day, Auburn traveled to Athens for the first time following a series of 18 games with Georgia played in either Atlanta, Macon, Montgomery, or Savannah. The city of Athens and the university were unusually warm and enthusiastic in greeting the Auburn team and its visiting supporters. Combining this with the supposed appeal of the newly constructed Sanford Field, it was hoped that the game would become an annual event in Athens.

Despite Georgia's home-field advantage, Auburn was favored to win by 3–2 odds. Surprisingly, a heavy snow fell the day before, and the field was covered with slushy, melting snow by the start of the game. Paddock must have felt right at home.

McWhorter and Hugh Conklin scored touchdowns for Georgia. Auburn could muster only two field goals by J.P. Major in a 12–6 Red and Black victory. Notably, within 20 minutes of the game's end, McWhorter was selected captain for the following season's team. He became the first UGA athlete to be named captain of both the football and baseball squads in the same calendar year.

Georgia's six-point victory over Auburn was much more decisive than the final score suggested. The victors held a 20–7 advantage in first downs and punted just six times compared to Auburn's 11. Although he did not score, Paddock had directed Georgia to an improbable victory in weather he was much more accustomed to than the Southern boys he guided and faced. The former halfback who barely made the Red and Black's team in 1912 would subsequently be selected two seasons later as Georgia's second All-American.

Getting Amends and Revenge

Georgia hosted an exceptional Virginia team on October 23, 1915, which would eventually finish the season with an 8–1 record. The Red and Black entered the contest undefeated but only a year removed from its lone losing season from 1910 to 1924. Georgia wouldn't have another losing season until 1926.

Georgia unexpectedly scored first when Bill Powell intercepted a pass and sped 80 yards for a touchdown. Powerhouses Yale and Harvard had combined to score just one touchdown against the same Cavaliers. Virginia answered with a touchdown of its own but missed the point after. Georgia led 7–6 late in the game and could sense a major upset.

After Virginia reached Georgia's 15-yard line late in the game, the field judge reportedly announced that only five seconds remained in the contest. The Cavaliers ran an additional play where Buck Mayer ran the width of the field and was knocked out of bounds for no gain. Virginia immediately lined up to attempt a field goal from Georgia's 20-yard line. As R.E. Tippett's kick was in the air, the timekeeper's whistle blew signaling the end of the game. However, since the play had already begun prior to the whistle being blown, Tippett's kick, which barely made it over the crossbar, counted, and the Cavaliers prevailed 9–7.

The Georgia followers were shocked and bewildered. They doubted that Virginia could run two plays, one where the player ran the width of the field, in just five seconds. To make matters worse, some in attendance contended that Tippett's game-winning attempt was, in fact, no good. Georgia's heart had been broken, a break that would necessitate considerably more time to heal because the Red and Black also lost the following week to Auburn 12–0.

Georgia traveled to Charlottesville, Virginia, the next season seeking amends and revenge against the Cavaliers. Despite the Red and Black once again being undefeated and Virginia having lost to Yale 61–3 two weeks before, Georgia was considered a slight underdog.

At a time when it was common for referees to be ex-players barely removed from their playing days, McWhorter, Georgia's first

All-American, served as the game's head linesman. He would show no favoritism toward Georgia, however. He had also coached previously at Virginia while attending its law school.

Although missing two of its best linemen, Georgia scored first when E.H. Dezendorf returned a fumbled punt 30 yards for a touchdown. Virginia later retaliated, and Georgia found itself behind 7–6 in the second quarter. Georgia recaptured the lead before halftime, when Dezendorf completed a 20-yard scoring pass to E.B. Tate.

Late in the game, Dezendorf attempted to field a Virginia punt near midfield. He fumbled, and Virginia's Charles Churchman picked up the loose ball and began racing toward the goal line. Just as it appeared the Red and Black would lose a second consecutive heartbreaking game to the Cavaliers, according to writer Howell Foreman, Georgia's "[Owen] Reynolds dived into Churchman's knees, runner and tackler fell within the shadow of the posts" at the Red and Black's 3-yard line. Virginia had enough time to run one final play, but a Dezendorf interception secured a 13–7 Georgia victory and avenged the Cavaliers' fortunate win from the season before.

Georgia students back home in Athens had packed the chapel to hear telegraphic returns of details on the game. They were ecstatic about the victory and displayed it a little differently than they would now as "the Georgia students celebrated the victory over Virginia [that night] in a great pajama parade."

Fitting End of an Era

Following Georgia's breathtaking win over Virginia in 1916, its season went into a tailspin. The Red and Black lost three of their next four games, including an October 28 meeting against Navy at Annapolis, Maryland. This was Georgia's first ever "intersectional" game, where it traveled outside of the Southeast.

The Red and Black finished the season against Alabama without two of its starting players—Reynolds and W.H. McLaws. The game was played at Birmingham's Rickwood Field with nearly

6,000 in attendance. The "Thin Red Line" of Alabama had begun the season by winning its first six contests but had dropped its last two games to Tulane and Georgia Tech.

The season finale for both squads began with no team mounting any kind of substantial drive for more than a few plays. At one point in the second stanza, Georgia started to move the ball. Halfbacks Dezendorf and John Coleman, who was expected to miss the game due to injury, advanced the team to Alabama's 35-yard line. From there, and with Dezendorf holding, William Donnelly, aided by a slight wind, kicked a field goal. Donnelly had missed a kick from the 45-yard line earlier in the ballgame.

The rest of the game was a punting duel between the two teams until Alabama advanced inside Georgia's 15-yard line late in the contest. Jake Taylor tore through the defense and nearly scored until he fumbled at the 5-yard line. Donnelly dove under an Alabama player to recover the fumble and rescue Georgia from defeat.

Georgia held the 3–0 lead and improved its all-time record over Alabama in Birmingham to 5–1–1. In victory, Donnelly's field goal and game-winning fumble recovery were a fitting end to an era of Georgia football that would soon experience a hiatus.

By the fall of 1917, most of the 1916 team was no longer playing football for Georgia, instead helping France defend the Western Front in World War I. The Red and Black's schedule was cancelled, and the university's football program would lay dormant for both the 1917 and 1918 seasons.

chapter 4
Achieving National Exposure and Recognition

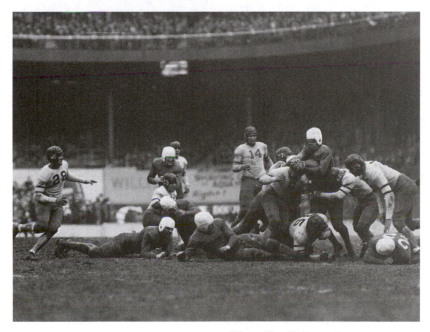

The Bulldogs' games against teams from the Northeast, including this game against New York University in 1929, helped to give the program national exposure. Photo courtesy of Bettman/CORBIS.

Remembering the Red and Black Stars

More than 125,000 United States soldiers were killed in World War I. This included five members of Georgia's 1916 football team: Tom Reed Beasley, Elliot Muse Braxton, Walter Hill Levie, Macon Caldwell Overton, and Edmund Brewer Tate.

Twenty years later, these war heroes were remembered and honored when Georgia hosted Tulane on November 13, 1937. A gathering at the University's Memorial Hall was held, including players from Georgia's 1910 through 1919 teams. During the benediction and in remembrance of the football players who gave their lives for their country, registrar Tom Reed unforgettably said:

They are not dead.
For such as they, there is no death.
The stars go down to rise upon some fairer shore.

The Ultimate Transfer

It had been nearly three years since Georgia played a football game when it opened the 1919 season against Citadel. Only four of Georgia's starting 11 had previously played college football, but most of the newcomers had post–high school football experience somewhere during the war, whether at Camp Hancock outside of Augusta, the Georgia Military Academy, or other places. Nevertheless, Coach Alex Cunningham expressed some concerns prior to Georgia's opener against a subpar Citadel team: "As the lineup shows, there is no nucleus of veterans to give the praise needed in case Citadel shows unexpected strength."

Halfback James Reynolds, tackle John Rigdon, and guard Artie Pew returned from Georgia's 1916 squad, which had a fairly successful 6–3 season. In addition, veteran A.M. "Bum" Day would play center for Georgia after being selected an All-American at Georgia Tech in 1918.

After high school, Day wanted to attend and play football at the University of Georgia. However, 1918 was the second year that football was cancelled at Georgia because of World War I. Day did not want to delay beginning his higher education and playing college football and consequently decided to enroll at Georgia Tech.

At Georgia Tech, Day was part of a Golden Tornado squad that, besides a loss to Pittsburgh, easily defeated every team on its schedule. Georgia Tech won six of seven games, outscoring its opponents 466–32. Day earned first team center on Walter Camp's All-American team. Despite personal and team accomplishments, Day immediately transferred to Georgia when it was announced the Red and Black would field a football team in 1919.

Day's presence was felt immediately in practices as Georgia prepared for the opening game. "He has shown an uncanny ability to diagnose formations and plays and to keep the line charging at all times…. Great confidence is placed in him, and he is regarded as a fit man to assist captain Pew to hold that line to the task," said Cunningham.

In the season opener, most of the 3,000 fans gave the Georgia team a thunderous ovation when it appeared on Sanford Field for the first time in three seasons. The spectators had each paid an admittance fee of only $1 with no reserved seating. Day would not only play center for Georgia but was also kicking on the opening kickoff.

Reynolds ran for a 30-yard score in the second quarter, while fullback Walter Neville scored two touchdowns. Although Georgia may have been "green," it defeated Citadel convincingly 28–0. The *Constitution* bragged that "for the first time in two years the Red and Black was represented by a team on the gridiron, and although some of the players lacked experience, they showed their ability to fight with the old Georgia spirit."

Day would letter for the next three seasons at Georgia and was named All-Southern Conference in 1920 and 1921. More than 60 years after his collegiate career, Day was curiously selected into the Athletics Hall of Fame at Georgia Tech—the school from which he transferred to pursue greener pastures at the University of Georgia.

Special Teams Wins Championship

In 1920, Herman Stegeman's first season as head coach, Georgia began the year undefeated with a 6–0–1 record. They faced an unscathed Alabama (8–0) team on November 20 for the SIAA championship. The game was played at Atlanta's Ponce de Leon Ball Park, then home of the Atlanta Crackers, a minor league baseball club. Although Georgia had an outstanding defensive team, its offense was considered questionable despite the team's undefeated record. Now nicknamed the Bulldogs after beginning the season as the Wildcats, Georgia had not allowed a single touchdown all season, mostly because of the play from its famous line. Known as the Stonewall Brigade whose motto was "They Shall Not Pass," the line featured ends Owen Reynolds and Paige Bennett, tackles Pew and Joe Bennett, guards Hollis Vandiver and Puss Whelchel, and center Bum Day.

Although it had allowed only one touchdown in its first eight games, Alabama was known for its proficient offense, which was averaging more than 37 points per contest. The Thin Red Line had scored the game's only points in its previous meeting with Georgia, winning 6–0 on two field goals by Talty O'Connor.

On the opening drive in a battle of the undefeated, Alabama's Mully Lenoir lost a fumble in midair. Bennett caught the ball and streaked 45 yards for a touchdown. On 'Bama's next possession, Whelchel blocked a punt, and Pew took it in for a score. Surprisingly, the Bulldogs had a 14–0 lead within the game's first three minutes of play.

On a 1-yard run, Lenoir scored for Alabama on the first play of the second quarter. It was the first touchdown against Georgia and its Stonewall Brigade in 10 games dating back to mid-November of the previous season. In the third period, Riggs Stephenson completed an 80-yard scoring pass to Al Clemens. O'Connor's point after tied the score 14–14.

Midway in the final quarter, Alabama reached Georgia's 18-yard line but then lost two yards on the next three plays. As O'Connor lined up to attempt a game-winning field goal, some of the crowd headed toward the exits, believing the accurate kicker would not miss.

O'Connor's kick was blocked by Whelchel and picked up by Buck Cheves, who then sprinted 82 yards for a Georgia touchdown. The Bulldogs led 21–14 while Stephenson was forced to punt on Alabama's final two possessions of the game. Georgia had won one of the most anticipated and spectacular games played in the South to that point. The victory still remains one of the school's most acclaimed.

Alabama finished the game with more yards (291–155), first downs (8–5), and offensive plays (86–58). The Crimson Tide beat Georgia in every facet of the game except the special teams play and the final score. In the words of writer Morgan Blake: "The Crimson crossed Georgia's goal line twice, but the men of Xen Scott [Alabama's head coach] were unequal to the task of winning. Alabama made two touchdowns, but Georgia made three, and three touchdowns will beat two touchdowns in any game played anywhere under the Stars and Stripes."

No Pushover

After Stegeman became Georgia's 16th head football coach, a movement was initiated to achieve greater national visibility for the football program. It was believed this could be accomplished by scheduling intersectional opponents, or opposition that belonged to a conference—Georgia would not join a conference until 1921—or was an independent outside of the Southeast. The Red and Black had traveled to Annapolis, Maryland, to face Navy in 1916, but, according to author Charles Martin, the "real invasion" occurred when Georgia journeyed to Cambridge, Massachusetts, to play Harvard in 1921.

By the 1920s, Harvard University had a strong football tradition, second only to Yale. The Crimson had won seven national championships from 1890 to 1919. Entering the game against Georgia on October 15, 1921, Harvard was unbeaten in 23 consecutive contests. Despite Harvard's football tradition and success, Georgia was confident it could upset the Crimson as 23 Bulldog players, Steadman Sanford, and coaches Stegeman, Jimmy DeHart, and Larry Conover embarked on their trip to Cambridge.

Some pregame reports suggested Harvard was overconfident prior to its matchup with Georgia and considered the game to be a practice session for the following week's contest against Penn State. However, Boston writers were surprised by how good Georgia looked in workouts leading up to the game. They were of the opinion that football in the South was not equal to that played in the East. Some of the writers were beginning to change their views and felt that Georgia could possibly win if they did not suffer "stage fright" playing in front of the 25,000 spectators who would be in attendance at Harvard Stadium.

In the most significant intersectional game of the college football season, Harvard scored within the first three minutes on a blocked punt returned for a touchdown. The Crimson later kicked a field goal and had a 10–0 halftime lead.

Midway through the final quarter, Georgia amazingly scored a touchdown on "a forward pass that followed a double pass" from Dave Collings to James Reynolds to Dick Hartley. Those were the first points Harvard had surrendered in seven games dating back to the previous season. Hartley had become the first southern player ever to cross the Crimson's goal line. At the same time, Georgia Tech was hosting Furman in Atlanta, and the Georgia-Harvard score was being kept on Grant Field's scoreboard. When Georgia's touchdown was indicated, Georgia Tech fans cheered while the Tech band played "Glory to Old Georgia." This may have been the first and last time that Georgia Tech supporters rooted and cheered for Georgia.

Newspapers declared Harvard was fortunate to defeat Georgia in a 10–7 Crimson victory. Harvard's offense did not score a touchdown during the entire game and was unable to move the ball in the second half, advancing only as far as Georgia's 40-yard line. The Bulldogs may have lost the game, but as writer Cliff Wheatley wrote "The glory of the victory was not to go to the players that triumphed…and finally to the southern team that came up to justify football in the South and who succeeded better than any Dixie team that has ever attempted the crusade."

Worthy Losses

Six weeks after Georgia's visit to Harvard in 1921 the Bulldogs played their second intersectional game of the season when they met Dartmouth at Atlanta's Grant Field. Although not as distinguished as Ivy League football powers Yale and Harvard, the Big Green of Dartmouth had an extraordinary .787 winning percentage since 1901.

Dartmouth left the Polo Grounds in New York following its game with Syracuse and traveled straight to Atlanta, having the luxury of nearly a full week of practice in preparation for its game with Georgia on November 26. On the other hand, the Bulldogs had to play a game two days prior to their contest against the Big Green.

On Thanksgiving Day in Athens, Georgia easily handled Clemson 28–0. The Bulldogs' starters played only the first quarter and a half, leaving the game with a 21–0 lead. Georgia departed Athens the following afternoon, spent Friday night in Atlanta, and had to be prepared for the 2:00 start on Saturday against Dartmouth. It was reported that practically every University of Georgia student and resident of Athens made the trip to Atlanta for the last college football game of the season in the South.

Despite the Big Green having ample time to prepare for the Bulldogs, who did not even get to practice in Atlanta, Georgia was considered a slight favorite. The game was a defensive battle from the onset, with both teams held scoreless until late in the first half.

With less than a minute remaining until halftime, Dartmouth was forced to punt. However, an offside penalty on Georgia gave the Big Green a first down. On the next play, with only 30 seconds remaining, Georgia was caught off guard, and Jim Robertson completed a 64-yard touchdown pass to Edward Lynch.

Down 7–0, Georgia mounted a drive toward the end of the game, but Dick Hartley fumbled a pass he had caught deep in Dartmouth territory. The ball then rolled out of the end zone for a

Big Green touchback. On Georgia's final drive, Hartley lost another fumble, and Dartmouth held on for the victory.

In 1922 Georgia faced the University of Chicago at Stagg Field. Georgia's Coach Stegeman, a Chicago alumnus, was just a few years removed from his playing days under the Maroons' legendary coach, Amos Alonzo Stagg. Currently a Division III football program, Chicago had regularly been a leader in the Big Ten Conference and was the heavy favorite over Georgia.

The meeting, but not necessarily the final score of the game, against the Maroons was of the utmost importance to Georgia as revealed in the *Constitution*: "The trip to Harvard last year was an epoch in the football history of Georgia, and just as this trip last year was of much importance, so will be the trip to Chicago." The train that took the Georgia team to Chicago also included 13 coaches of Bulldogs followers.

As was the case against Harvard and Dartmouth in the previous season, Georgia was defeated by Chicago. Nevertheless, the Bulldogs had begun to play schools outside of the southeastern United States and gained national exposure and an enhanced reputation in the process. Georgia was still without a victory over an intersectional opponent, but it would be only a matter of time until it finally triumphed over a distinguished team from the North.

Tiebreaker

Following Georgia's 1917 and 1918 suspended seasons, its series with Georgia Tech was set to resume. That is, until it was cancelled because of an incident that began at, of all sports, a baseball game.

"General misbehavior" at a Georgia–Georgia Tech baseball game between both schools' fans on May 9, 1919, started the dispute. Just two days following the signing of a supposed "peace treaty" by the two student bodies, conflict erupted again. At Georgia's annual Senior Parade, banners were displayed insinuating that, while Georgia Tech was home playing football during the 1917 and 1918 seasons, Georgia players were off fighting in the war. Georgia Tech was outraged, and its athletics director demanded a public apology from the University of Georgia senior class. Georgia refused. The end result would be no scheduled athletic events between the two schools for six years.

Athletics director Sanford of Georgia and J.B. Crenshaw of Georgia Tech, resumed athletic relations on March 1, 1924, in a reinstated rivalry depicted by writer Cliff Wheatley as, "When Georgia and Georgia Tech meet in athletic endeavors, be the game of shuffleboard or football...anything is likely to happen." A football game between the two schools finally took place in the fall of 1925, with Georgia Tech defeating the Bulldogs 3–0.

In 1926 Georgia was having a mediocre season prior to its meeting with Georgia Tech. George Woodruff was in his fourth year as head coach and, along with assistants Harry Mehre and Jim Crowley, had led the Bulldogs to a 4–3 year prior to the Tech contest. The Yellow Jackets were one game worse with a record of 3–4 and perceived as the underdog.

Before a sold-out Grant Field, Georgia Tech scored 13 points in the second quarter on a Bob Horn scoring run and a Sam Murray touchdown pass. After the second score, Murray's conversion attempt was blocked by Georgia's Ivy "Chick" Shiver. This turned out to be an all-important mishap.

Early in the second half, the Bulldogs began their resurgence. Herdis McCrary dashed 26 yards for a touchdown following a fumble recovery by Bob Morris. It was the first time points were scored by Georgia against the Golden Tornado since Steve Crump rushed for two touchdowns 13 years earlier. In the final quarter, Georgia's George Morton threw a 35-yard touchdown pass to Jack Curran to tie the game at 13 points. It was Curran's only touchdown in his career as a Bulldog. Roy Johnson's successful point after broke the tie and would be the difference in breaking a tied series. Georgia's 14–13 victory was described as "the most spectacular, the most thrilling, and most colorful football game ever witnessed in Georgia football history" and gave the Bulldogs a 10–9–2 series lead over their in-state rival.

After the game a sight reportedly never witnessed in Atlanta was evident on Grant Field. A large portion of the 33,000 in attendance stormed the field and cheered while milling about the grounds. The fans were said to be of all types, from Bulldog to Yellow Jacket followers, toddlers to students, and from lawyers to preachers.

Finally!

Georgia began its 1927 season by dismantling Virginia in Athens 32–0. Next on the schedule was Yale. For the fifth consecutive season, Georgia would travel to New Haven, Connecticut, to play in the Yale Bowl.

The Bulldogs had lost all eight of their previous intersectional games, including four to Yale by a combined score of 101–13. However, the '27 squad, known later as the "Dream and Wonder Team," was one of Georgia's best to date and would eventually contend for a national title. Also, Yale apparently had been weaker of late than it had been in years past, recording a 4–4 record the previous season. This was only the second time in their 55-year history the Elis had lost four or more games.

A victory by Georgia would not only garner prestige for its football program but for southern football in general. Georgia had an experienced and healthy team, and, to the Bulldogs' liking, New Haven was experiencing unusually warm weather. Coach George "Kid" Woodruff was fairly confident in his squad, as he indicated the following a couple of days prior to the skirmish: "We are going to New Haven to give Tad Jones [Yale's coach] and his crew all we have, and we intend to do our best to win. We are after victory, and if it is possible we will get it." However, the Blue was a 14-point favorite, and a Bulldog win was thought to be inconceivable.

Yale fumbled on its first offensive play, and the ball was recovered by Georgia's Herdis McCrary. Soon afterward, as the Eli crowd chanted "Hold 'em Yale," H.F. Johnson tossed a 12-yard touchdown to Chick Shiver. Yale would tie the game at 7–7 and kick a field goal in the second quarter to take a 10–7 lead. Late in the first half, McCrary scored on a 2-yard rush following a 59-yard pass from Bobby Hooks to Frank Dudley. Georgia led 14–10 at halftime.

Yale blew several scoring opportunities in the first three quarters and was in scoring position four times in the fourth quarter: the Blue were held on downs on Georgia's 1-yard line; Dudley intercepted an Eli pass; Yale caught a pass behind the goal line, but Georgia drove the player out of the end zone for an incompletion; and Bulldog Gene Smith recovered a Yale fumble inside Georgia's 10-yard line.

Georgia had accomplished the improbable and defeated an intersectional northern power on its own turf. Coach Woodruff was given much praise, as the *Journal* wrote that the Kid "inspired the most courageous Georgia outfit in history to storm the impenetrable heights and defeat Yale, 14–10, in as thrilling a contest as has been staged in the famous bowl in all its years."

Like "Mother Foley," Like Son

After Georgia's momentous victory over Yale in 1927, the Bulldogs defeated Furman the following week 32–0. On October 22, 1927, the undefeated Bulldogs faced Auburn in neutral Columbus, Georgia. Auburn kicked a field goal in the first quarter, but Georgia responded with 27 second-quarter points.

The most elated person at the game reportedly was A.L. Foley, or "Mother Foley," a 69-year-old woman who had two sons attend the University of Georgia. She was considered "the staunchest supporter the Bulldogs have ever had." During halftime, she turned to writer W.C. Munday and said that Georgia's performance in its 24-point lead was the finest sight in the world that there ever was.

After the Bulldogs' 33–3 victory, Mother Foley was surprised by a visit from assistant coach Harry Mehre, who gave her the game ball. Tearfully, Foley said to Mehre, "Really, Harry, you've made me happier than I've ever been, and I do not know how to express my appreciation." Wiping her tears and undaunted, Foley continued, "By the way, how about putting your name on this ball?" Mehre obliged, and subsequently head coach Woodruff and assistant Jim Crowley also added their autographs.

Mother Foley must have passed her avid loyalty to Georgia to her son, Frank. Frank Foley was a standout baseball player on Georgia's 1908 championship team and later was instrumental in bringing the Georgia-Auburn game to Columbus every year. The university's baseball stadium, Foley Field, is named after him.

Girls, Fishing, and Oconee River Juice

On Thursday, October 27, 1927, the Bulldogs traveled to New Orleans, Louisiana, for the first time to play Tulane that Saturday. Thirty-two players and nine others, including coaches, trainers, and newspaper writers, boarded the Piedmont Limited train at 2:45 PM in Atlanta bound for Bay St. Louis, Mississippi, located 50 miles from New Orleans.

On Friday morning, the entire train awoke to guard Gene "Jug Head" Smith hollering for someone to loan him a shaving razor. Soon after the train stopped in Bay St. Louis, 10 passengers, including Whitner Cary of the *Constitution*, decided to go fishing. Just as the group set off to fish, two attractive girls driving a sports roadster pulled up to the group. It was only moments until half the party, including Shiver and Glenn Lautzenhiser, were sitting comfortably in the car with the girls. The other half continued to fish, catching only two flounder, two drums, and an eel between them. The Bulldogs proved to Cary that they were "bearcats with the girls" but "the worst fishermen in the conference."

Georgia coaches worried that the long trip and hot climate would take its toll on the team. They also feared, for whatever reason, that the water of New Orleans would have an ill effect on the squad. Because this concerned the coaches, "some 10 gallons of Oconee river juice" from Athens was brought on the journey.

Something must have been in Georgia's homegrown "juice," or maybe it was inspiration drawn from the two girls in the car, because the Bulldogs easily trounced Tulane 31–0.

chapter 5

Mehre Makes His Mark

Coach Harry Mehre (center), along with various other ex–Notre Dame players who became his assistants over the years, helped to institute Knute Rockne's football philosophies in the South.
Photo courtesy of Bettmann/Corbis.

A Grand Opening

In 1927 Dr. Steadman Sanford, faculty chairman of athletics, began a crusade to bring a modern stadium to the University of Georgia. Donators pledged at least $1,000 against an $180,000 loan from the Trust Company of Georgia for the construction. In return, contributors received the right to purchase six tickets inside the new stadium's 40-yard lines. The architects chosen had previously designed North Carolina's Kenan Stadium and the Yale Bowl. The site chosen was a large ravine between the university's college of agriculture and Franklin College.

Sanford wanted Yale to be the team Georgia hosted for the stadium's dedication for several reasons. For one, the Elis were college football's most traditional power. Also, Georgia had established an athletic relationship with Yale, playing against the Blue in New Haven, Connecticut, for six consecutive seasons (1923–1928). Sanford's colleagues doubted that Yale, never having traveled to play a team not from the East, would venture as far south as Athens. However, Sanford strenuously worked with southern Yale alumni, and the Elis eventually accepted his invitation.

On October 12, 1929, on the third home game of the season, Georgia hosted Yale for the dedication of Sanford Stadium. People began arriving in Athens for the historical event three days before the game, and the town quickly filled with a circus-like atmosphere. Hotel vacancies completely disappeared, while seats at the new stadium filled up so quickly that aisle space started to be sold.

A day before the game, the *Constitution* described the scene: "The greatest show of the year is already starting. The yelp of the crowd can already be heard...and the hysteria will have full sway. [Harry] Mehre [Georgia's coach] plans to keep them [Georgia players] in a quiet spot—if one can be found."

Thousands of automobiles and 40 trains arrived in the small college town. Most of the traveling patrons coming from considerable distances were forced to lodge in Atlanta. Some were fortunate to stay with Athens citizens in a number of private homes opened to visitors. In a town of 15,000 residents, 35,000 fans were expected to jam into Sanford Stadium. Among the prominent citizens attending were four governors, including New York's Franklin D. Roosevelt, who would become president of the United States four years later. Since a planned dedication ceremony of 15 minutes preceded the 2:00 kickoff, printed on each ticket was the request, "Please be in your seat at 1:45, Eastern time."

Georgia had a young and inexperienced squad, with eight sophomores starting. They had been upset in their season opener against Oglethorpe University, but had recovered to shut out Furman University 27-0. Yale had crushed Vermont 89–0 in its first game. Who would win was anyone's guess. Most people believed the contest to be a toss-up.

"Catfish" and Fellow Dogs 3–0 vs. Elis

The fun surrounding Sanford Stadium's dedication, from the enormous crowd to the excitement to the ambiance, were all that was anticipated plus much more. Everything, that is, but the final score.

In the second quarter Georgia's Jack Roberts and Red Maddox, two of the Bulldogs' eight sophomore starters, blocked Yale punts. Sophomore end Vernon "Catfish" Smith fell on the ball in the end zone for a touchdown. Smith would add the point after, and Georgia would lead at halftime 7–0.

In the third quarter a punt by Smith was downed on Yale's 14-yard line. In turn, the Elis attempted to punt safely out of their end of the field on first down. It's necessary to note that prior to football teams fully utilizing the passing game, which resulted in offenses becoming more productive, punting before the fourth down was fairly common. The Blue's snapped ball sailed over Albie Booth and into the end zone. Booth retrieved the ball and attempted to run it out over the goal line. However, with Smith closing in for a tackle, Booth was forced to go out of bounds before he made it out of the end zone. Georgia had scored a safety and led 9–0.

In the final quarter Smith scored again when he caught a pass from Spurgeon Chandler, another sophomore and an MVP in

Major League Baseball 14 years later. Georgia would hold its comfortable lead and record its second victory over Yale in remarkable fashion. Bill Fincher wrote: "Georgia, a more or less floundering team in its first two games, seemed a wonderfully coordinated machine against Yale. With the whole Georgia team in star roles, Vernon Smith covered himself with glory."

Georgia certainly did not flounder in its dedication of Sanford Stadium versus one of college football's elite. Instead, a Catfish was responsible for all of the Bulldogs' points in a 15–0 victory.

Georgia's young "Flaming Sophomores" of 1929 had a respectable 6–4 record, having defeated Yale, Auburn, Alabama, and Georgia Tech, along with handing North Carolina its only loss of the season. The Bulldogs followed that with a 7–2–1 campaign in 1930. Victories included contests against North Carolina, Auburn, New York University, and Yale again, while Georgia's two losses were against teams that would finish the season with a combined 18–1 record. Much was expected from Georgia in 1931, as Smith, Maddox, Chandler, quarterback Austin Downes, and the rest of the class were experienced seniors. They had a difficult schedule, however, including another trip to play Yale in New Haven.

Prior to the '31 Yale game, Morgan Blake of the *Journal* curiously stated, "If Georgia gets an even break in officiating, which would be a very rare event in that section [the eastern United States], the Athens Bulldogs will bring home the bacon again." Georgia was seeking its fourth win over Yale in five seasons.

Smith had become well known to the Elis and eastern football fans because of his performances against Yale the previous two seasons. Interestingly, he, along with Downes, made an unusual appearance on the Bridgeport, Connecticut, radio station WICC the day before the game. That must have been some thrill for those two southern boys!

The Bulldogs whipped the Blue 26–7 in front of 75,000 in the Yale Bowl. Smith caused a fumble that was returned by Red Leathers for Georgia's first score. The other radio guest, Downes, was referred to afterward by Yale's coach, Mal Stevens, as the best quarterback he had ever seen play in the Blue's home stadium. Smith was said to have played the game of his career and "was known to everyone at the bowl," according to the *Journal*. "He was jeered, and he was cheered. The jeering was good natured, the cheering sincere."

In Athens before the game ended, university freshmen began gathering boxes, paper, furniture, and any other flammable material to start an enormous bonfire on Herty Field. The fire was ignited at 8:00 PM. A big pajama and shirt-tail parade through downtown preceded the lighting. When the triumphant Bulldogs arrived in town two nights later, they were accorded the biggest reception ever given to a Georgia team.

Believe It or Mott

Georgia began its 1930 season by hosting Oglethorpe University in Athens on September 27. The Flaming Sophomores of '29 were experienced juniors, and Georgia now had a veteran starting lineup. At practice two days prior to the season opener, one underclassman, halfback Norman "Buster" Mott, was identified as the only newcomer to break into the Bulldogs' starting 11. Mott had demonstrated a knack for breaking off large rushing gains from scrimmage.

On the day of the game, coach Harry Mehre decided to take no chances against the Petrels because Georgia had been upset by Oglethorpe the prior season 13–7. He inserted all veterans into his starting lineup, and Mott was designated as a second-string halfback.

Georgia's veterans jumped out to a quick 18–0 lead midway in the second quarter. Feeling comfortable with the three-touchdown advantage, Mehre inserted the second team, including Mott, into the game. On its ensuing possession, Oglethorpe was held on downs. Georgia took over, and in the game's next two possessions, according to writer Ralph McGill, "Sophomore Buster Mott, winging down the field like a harried ghost, broke the Petrels' heart[s] with two amazing runs for touchdowns."

Immediately after Georgia took over on downs on its own 40-yard line, Mott broke loose for a 60-yard scoring run aided by the blocking of guard Jimmy Patterson. On the very next series, Oglethorpe was intercepted by Mott. Following blocks by Tommy Moran, Buster returned the errant pass 51 yards for another touchdown.

The Bulldogs now led 31–0 and eventually would defeat the Petrels 31–6. The decisive victory over Oglethorpe was accomplished, despite having two fewer first downs (14–12) and only 48 more total yards (238–190).

Mott was later featured in *Ripley's Believe It or Not!* for scoring long touchdowns the first two times he handled the ball as a Georgia Bulldog. Surprising no one, a week after defeating Oglethorpe, Mehre decided that Mott was more valuable in the starting lineup, and the newcomer started against Mercer at one of the halfback positions.

An Old System in a New Conference

In 1933 Mehre was serving his sixth season of a 10-year tenure as the head coach at Georgia. As was the case with most schools in the South, it was quite an accomplishment for the university to have the same football coach for more than just a brief period. In its first 18 years of football, Georgia had 14 different head coaches, none of whom coached for more than two seasons.

Prior to the 1920s, there were very few sufficiently trained coaches who were willing to guide a southern team. The salary was extremely low, and the job lasted only a few months.

In 1910 Alex Cunningham was hired at Georgia and broke the trend by coaching the team for eight seasons, from 1910 to 1919. Cunningham had no assistants coaching under him. He was a one-man show, guiding and instructing the entire team by himself. Herman Stegeman (1920–1922) and George Woodruff (1923–1927) were the first Georgia coaches to utilize multiple assistants.

In the mid-1920s, Mehre, Frank Thomas, and Jim Crowley were notable assistant coaches at Georgia. Under the guidance of the great coach, Knute Rockne, all three had been standout players at Notre Dame. In fact, Crowley was a member of its famed Four Horsemen from 1922 to 1924. When these three assistants arrived at Georgia, they brought with them the discipline and tactics of Coach Rockne, including the "Rockne system." This included a cadence for a shifting backfield, which could confuse the opposition while opening holes in the line for large gains.

About the time Mehre was promoted from assistant to Georgia's head coach in 1928, both Thomas and Crowley began very successful head-coaching careers of their own. Soon afterward, Mehre hired Rex Enright and Ted Twomey. Both assistants had also starred at Notre Dame in the 1920s and were quite familiar with the Rockne system.

In 1933 Georgia had left the crowded, 23-member Southern Conference and joined, along with 12 other schools, the new Southeastern Conference. As was the case for the previous several seasons, the Bulldogs would continue to employ the Rockne system in their new conference.

Backs Cy Grant, Homer Key, and George Chapman excelled in the system's shifting-cadence backfield during the 1933 season. For the year, Grant scored eight touchdowns and 58 total points while Chapman added six scores. All three backs were eventually selected on either the second or third teams of the SEC's all-conference squads.

Georgia began that season with seven consecutive wins and was in first place in the Southeastern Conference. The Bulldogs were ranked number two in the nation prior to a 14–6 loss to Auburn. Against Georgia Tech, a 79-yard touchdown pass from Key to Grant and a successful point after by Grant was the difference in a 7–6 victory over the rival Yellow Jackets.

"Stadium Rocking, Girders Are Bending Now..."

After opening the 1934 season with a 42–0 win over Stetson University, Georgia traveled to Greenville, South Carolina, to face Furman on October 6. Before and throughout the game, Furman's

Manley Field endured powerful winds and constant rain, leaving the gridiron wet and heavily muddied.

The Bulldogs slipped and sloshed their way to a 7–2 lead late in the contest. Suddenly, a section of the west stands, seating 500 of the stadium's 3,000 in attendance, collapsed. While some fans in the stands were screaming, others were shouting for them to remain calm. Fortunately, only three spectators were injured, and only two had to be taken to the hospital. During the clamor, the game was never halted, and Georgia held its five-point advantage for the victory.

After the contest, writer Jimmy Jones described the chaotic scene at Manley Field and made light of the near tragedy: "The press box…trembled and swayed under the impact [of the stands collapsing] but the lofty structure…was supported by extra braces and remained secure, else this story would be written by a pinch-hitter."

Big-Play Bill

Prior to becoming a well-known backfield and volunteer kicking coach for decades at Georgia until the mid-1990s, during his playing days as a Bulldog Bill Hartman was considered one of the finest but most underrated all-around football players in college football. In particular, he is best known for his performances in two games in 1937, a year when he was Georgia's only first-team All-American in a five-season span (1936–1940).

In Mehre's final season as Georgia's head coach, 1937, Captain Hartman earned All-American recognition at fullback. However, in Georgia's eighth game of the season, against Tulane, on November 13, Hartman was the Bulldogs' starting quarterback in an offense that rarely threw the football.

Against Tulane, Georgia's offense was not throwing the ball and had difficulty running as well. Hartman was forced to punt 10 times in the first half and 17 times in total. Before halftime, half of his kicks were downed inside the opponent's 20-yard line, and Tulane garnered only one yard returning his punts. One of

Hartman's punts, which went out of bounds on the opponent's 2-yard line, led to Georgia's only score.

After being pinned near its own goal line, Tulane was forced to punt. Georgia's Vassa Cate fielded the Green Wave kick and dashed down the sideline for a 37-yard touchdown. Hartman held for Billy Mims's extra point attempt, which was successful.

Hartman's 17 punts averaged 40 yards per kick, including a 44-yard average in the first half. His punts included one kicked from his own 16-yard line to Tulane's 12. "It was a 72-yard kick," said Jack Troy of the *Constitution*. "A tremendous piece of punting by the Georgia captain, who was playing a magnificent game of football."

The Green Wave would score a touchdown in the final quarter, but their extra point was blocked. Despite gaining just one first down and netting minus-7 yards on offense, according to the *Constitution* (but four yards according to an Athens statistician), Georgia won 7–6 thanks to Cate's return and Hartman's stellar punting efforts.

Two weeks later, Georgia played Georgia Tech in the rain on a muddy Grant Field. Once again, the Bulldogs could not generate any offense, but the Yellow Jackets could not cross Georgia's goal line in a scoreless first half.

To start the third quarter, Bill Hartman fielded the Yellow Jackets' second-half kickoff at his own 7-yard line and streaked down the middle of the field for a 93-yard touchdown. It would be the only time Georgia would cross onto Georgia Tech's side of the 50-yard line. In the third quarter, the Yellow Jackets knotted the game at six points with a touchdown, but Georgia's Quinton Lumpkin blocked the point-after attempt to preserve the tie.

Georgia was extremely fortunate to tie Georgia Tech because the Bulldogs gained just two first downs and 49 total yards in the contest. Hartman rushed for only seven yards on seven carries but averaged 42 yards on 15 punts and scored Georgia's lone touchdown.

The Bulldogs were dubbed the "hitless wonders" by the media for their consecutive performances against Tulane, Auburn, and Georgia Tech. Georgia gained only a combined eight first downs and 167 total yards (0 passing) against the trio. Primarily because of Hartman's efforts, Georgia did not lose any of these games, defeating Tulane and tying both Auburn and Tech.

Everyone Should Experience the "Cocktail Party"

Georgia president Dr. Harmon Caldwell, director of athletics W.O. Payne, and former Georgia player and coach George Woodruff attended the Sugar Bowl in New Orleans on January 1, 1938. After Santa Clara had defeated LSU, the trio approached LSU assistant Joel Hunt request an interview. Following Mehre's departure from Georgia to coach Ole Miss, surprise replacement Hunt was named the Bulldogs' head coach and Wally Butts, a high school coach, to his assistant. Hunt was an all-purpose star player for Texas A&M in the mid-1920s and was tabbed by the legendary John Heisman as the greatest all-around player he had ever seen.

No longer would Georgia's offense be designed after Notre Dame's as Mehre had successfully done. Instead, Hunt implemented a single wingback offense. With the likes of Jim Fordham, Harry Stevens, and Vassa Cate, Georgia had an abundance of talent in the backfield under its first-year coach.

The team's talent was questioned, however, and Georgia fans suddenly became pessimistic during Hunt's first game. The Bulldogs were losing to Citadel at halftime but rallied to win 20–12. Some fans were disgruntled about the close score, considering that Citadel was supposed to be a far-inferior team.

Nevertheless, the Bulldogs won their first four games under Hunt before losing in Worcester, Massachusetts, to Holy Cross, which would finish the season ranked ninth in the nation by the Associated Press. This led to the first conference game of the season on November 5 with Florida, a preseason SEC title contender.

As are today's Georgia-Florida meetings, the game in 1938 was played in "neutral" Jacksonville, Florida, in a sold-out Fairfield Stadium, later known as the Gator Bowl and currently named Alltel Stadium. It would be nearly 20 years before the game was first referred to as the "World's Largest Outdoor Cocktail Party" or the "Cocktail Party," as it has been for years until recently, becasue of the two schools' concern and sensitivity regarding extensive alcohol consumption at the game. However, the Georgia-Florida game was also a major social event before it acquired what has recently been defined as a derogatory label by school administrators. At the 1938 meeting of the two schools, on the Friday before the game, fans filled "the air with music and cries of 'Fill 'em up again.'" It seems safe to speculate that the Georgia and Florida fans were not referring to filling up the gas tanks of their vehicles.

The Gators had upset the Bulldogs 6–0 the season before and had tied the game at six points in the fourth quarter in '38. Georgia broke the deadlock and eventually won 19–6, holding Florida to just 124 total yards. The Bulldogs completed only two of 11 passes, but the completions were 49- and 31-yard tosses by Billy Mims.

Joel Hunt's only Georgia-Florida contest was similar to the few that preceded it. Although the two teams were not particularly outstanding, the game and the entire weekend were certainly memorable, especially from a social aspect. Georgia recorded a 0–3–1 record in its final four games, and Hunt left Athens after a 5–4–1 season. And on just one occasion, he did experience the "Cocktail Party."

chapter 6

Arrival of the "Little Round Man" and "Fireball"

Wallace Butts was handpicked to be the head coach at Georgia after one year of college coaching experience. During his college days, Butts was a star player at Mercer.

A New Beginning with Butts

Former Georgia star player and head coach George "Kid" Woodruff insisted on the hiring of 34-year-old Wallace Butts for the head coaching position in 1939. Butts was Joel Hunt's assistant during the '38 season and a bona fide uncertainty to succeed at Georgia. Woodruff, a successful businessman in Columbus, Georgia, was a major financial contributor to the football program and had complete faith that Butts would excel as a coach. In fact, Woodruff indicated he would take full responsibility if the young coach failed.

Butts's first coaching staff included four Georgia lettermen— Spec Towns, Quinton Lumpkin, Bill Hartman, and Howell Hollis— and two future college head coaches—J.B. "Ears" Whitworth (Oklahoma A&M and Alabama) and J.V. Sikes (Kansas). The coaches put the players through rigorous preseason practices more strenuous and of longer duration than characteristic of previous seasons' sessions. The Bulldogs unexpectedly began to demonstrate exceptional blocking and hustling in their practices like never before.

Although the backfield was experienced and talented, with the likes of Vassa Cate, Jim Fordham, and Billy Mims, little was expected from the team in '39. Georgia's pass defense was a major concern since college teams were beginning to throw the football with more regularity. In previous seasons, an adequate pass defense was not necessary. As it turned out, Georgia's season opener was against Citadel and quarterback Graham Edwards, who was regarded as one of the South's best passers.

Injuries struck the team a few days prior to the game. Sophomore Heyward Allen, an excellent passer, was already lost for a few weeks after an appendectomy. Cate injured an ankle two days before the Citadel game, and it appeared that wingback Cliff Kimsey would miss the game because of an infected wisdom tooth. Georgia's wingback situation was in dire circumstances. The only healthy player at the position was Oliver Hunnicutt, and he, according to practice reports, "has been hampered throughout his college career by poor eyesight."

As Coach Butts began his first season in Athens, there seemed to be more questions than answers regarding his team's prognosis. Citadel was far from a guaranteed victory—it had almost defeated Georgia the year before en route to a six-win season. Bulldog fans were excited about the new Georgia team (wearing new uniforms) being coached by newcomer Wally Butts but realized it would take years before the Bulldogs once again would be among the South's elite. Johnny Bradberry of the *Constitution* wrote, "For Wallace Butts, stocky and amiable, has supporters more enthusiastic than at any time since the 'Flaming Sophomores of '29.' Not about this year's team but future 11s of Georgia's new deal on the gridiron."

Since ticket prices had been dropped to $1.10, and any high school student in the state of Georgia was admitted free of charge, 17,000 spectators filled Sanford Stadium for the Bulldogs' battle with Citadel. They witnessed Georgia, filled with "overanxiousness and spirited play" under its new coach, suffer 170 penalty yards but cruise to a 26–0 victory.

Butts's team outgained the opponent 463–72 in yardage, while Citadel's feared passing game completed six of 12 passes for only 36 yards and was intercepted on three occasions. Uncharacteristic of seasons past, Georgia passed for 131 yards on 18 attempts—a sign of things to come during the Butts era. The Bulldogs used 37 players in the win, including the "near-blind" Hunnicutt, who had a 30-yard run that was featured in a photo on the cover of the sports section of the *Constitution*.

Fabulous Freshmen

Wally Butts's first season at Georgia was far from a success. The Bulldogs' 5–6 record was their worst in seven years. However, there was another football team at the university that flourished in 1939—Georgia's "point-a-minute" freshman team.

Freshmen coaches Lumpkin and Hollis had a talented squad of 43 men, with depth at every position. A 68–0 victory over South Carolina was highlighted by two punts returned for scores by

Lamar Davis and three touchdown passes from Frank Sinkwich. Georgia Military College was also routed 65–6 as the Bullpups returned both a punt (Davis again) and a kick (Ken Keuper) for scores. In the contest, Georgia's frosh outrushed GMC 327 yards to three. In the 14th annual Georgia–Georgia Tech freshman game the Bullpups tied the series at seven wins for each school, with a 33–0 thrashing of the Baby Jackets. Booker Blanton rushed and passed for scores, and Davis scored another touchdown on a 51-yard reception from Jim Todd. As he had been for the entire freshman schedule, Sinkwich was again spectacular against the Jackets. Sinkwich, born in McKees, Pennsylvania, and who grew up in Youngstown, Ohio, rushed for 45- and 10-yard scores.

Let There Be Lights

For the 1940 season Sinkwich was considered one of Georgia football's key players despite being just a sophomore who had never seen varsity action. Sinkwich had large hips and walked pigeon-toed, characteristics not associated with a spectacular, fleet-footed halfback. When he first came to Georgia, someone pointed out Sinkwich to an assistant coach and declared he could be a potential gridiron star. Eyeing Sinkwich, the coach assumed he was joking.

Georgia began the '40 season by defeating Oglethorpe University and South Carolina by a combined 84 points but then suffered losses to talented Ole Miss and Columbia squads. Kentucky was next on the Bulldogs' schedule for the first night game ever at Georgia's Sanford Stadium. Georgia had played at night before on the road but never under the lights in Athens. Kickoff was set for Friday night at 7:15 "Atlanta time" on October 25.

En route to Athens from Kentucky, the Wildcats interestingly stopped off first at Georgia Tech in Atlanta. On Thursday night they practiced under the lights of Grant Field before leaving for Athens the morning of the game. The Wildcats would enter with an impressive 4–0–1 record. Similar to Georgia at one time, Ole

One of Georgia's all-time greats, Frank Sinkwich led some legendary Bulldog teams during the 1940s.

Miss (coached by Harry Mehre, former Georgia head coach), and South Carolina in 1940 (coached by Rex Enright, former Georgia assistant), Kentucky used Notre Dame's shifting offensive system. Many felt that Georgia's recent misfortune would soon change, but Kentucky was quite good and favored to hand the Bulldogs their third-consecutive loss.

At the time, Coach Wally Butts had a personal rivalry with Kentucky's head coach, A.D. Kirwan. The rivalry had begun several years earlier when both were high school coaches in Louisville, Kentucky—Butts at Male High and Kirwan at Du Pont Manual High. Butts had won two of three games from Kirwan when the two coached in high school, but Kirwan's Wildcats had defeated Georgia 13–6 in 1939.

Roughly 16,000 spectators invaded Sanford Stadium in, according to the *Journal*, "a game that officially brings night football to Athens. It is the first time in history that Georgia has entertained a gridiron foe under the arcs."

With a few minutes remaining in the game, Kentucky led 7–0 and Georgia had the ball on its own 49-yard line. Sophomore Sinkwich took over, completing two passes for a combined 33 yards on the drive and rushing for 18 yards on four carries. His last rush was a one-yard touchdown run with 2:23 remaining in the game. Leo Costa's point after tied the game, and the contest eventually ended in a 7–7 deadlock.

Georgia defeated the favored Wildcats in every phase of the game except in the number of points scored. Sinkwich's late-game drive was regarded as one of the finest "in Southern athletic history." The Bulldogs easily outgained Kentucky in yardage (309–159) and first downs (18–7) as Georgia's record stood at 2-2-1. Writer Ed Danforth was optimistic about the Bulldogs' future: "One of these days their luck will change, and when it does, look out…the dice will begin falling in sevens and 11s and it will be the making of the club."

When All Else Fails, Pass

After the tie with Kentucky in 1940, Georgia split its next two contests against Auburn and Florida. The "Fabulous Frosh," or the "point-a-minute" freshman team of '39, was now known, according to writer Jack Troy, as the "thrill-a-minute sophomores" despite their .500 record. The Bulldogs next traveled to New Orleans to face Tulane. The Green Wave were favored, especially because Georgia's sensational Sinkwich was hampered with an injured ankle.

Sinkwich was healthy enough to toss a first-quarter six-yard score to George Poschner to give Georgia a surprising 6–0 lead. Coach Wally Butts had never substituted a quarterback while coaching the Bulldogs, but his 1940 team was inexperienced and suffered many injuries. At one point, Butts replaced quarterback and alternative captain Robin Nowell with Sinkwich, the coach's star halfback.

Georgia still led 6–0 in the third quarter, when it found itself backed up near its own goal line. Quarterback Sinkwich called the play and unexpectedly dropped back in the end zone to pass, an extremely rare occurrence in the earlier days of college football. Sinkwich's pass was intercepted, and, two plays later, Tulane had reached the end zone. Despite Georgia's Lamar "Racehorse" Davis returning the ensuing kickoff for a 96-yard touchdown, the Green Wave scored two late touchdowns and went on to win 21–13.

Butts questioned Sinkwich's judgment regarding why he would throw the ball out of his own end zone. The self-assured and often direct halfback/quarterback answered, "Poor quarterbacking? Well, Coach, we tried to run it out. We couldn't run it out. We couldn't kick it out. Best thing to do, I thought, was to throw it out."

After the loss, Georgia's record dropped to 3–4–1. However, following a week off, the Bulldogs salvaged the season with a 21–19 victory over Georgia Tech and a win at Miami by three touchdowns. Butts, known as the "Little Round Man" because of his stature, and his squad had achieved a winning season in his second campaign. It seemed the Bulldogs' bad luck was beginning to fade.

A Win over the Ranked

On October 18, 1941, Georgia faced Columbia at New York's Baker Field. Both squads were undefeated, with the Lions ranked number 20 in the Associated Press poll. Since the initial poll for college football had begun in 1936, Georgia had played two ranked teams, tying number-three Fordham in 1936 and losing to number-19 New York University three years later.

Columbia had narrowly defeated the Bulldogs 19–13 the previous season. Entering the final quarter, Georgia had led 13–12 on two touchdown receptions by Davis thrown by Sinkwich and Heyward Allen. However, the Lions took a six-point lead they would not relinquish following a Leonard Will lateral to Phillip

Bayer for a 35-yard score. Photos by an Athens photographer would later indicate the winning touchdown was presumably the result of an illegal forward pass. Nevertheless, Georgia coach Wally Butts accepted the loss and commented that he did "not want to discredit Columbia's victory or alibi our [Georgia's] defeat."

The Lions had achieved their national ranking prior to their game with Georgia in '41 by shutting out a good Princeton team the previous week 21−0. At a time when only five college bowl games were played, it was known that Columbia was seeking a Rose Bowl berth, the most prestigious and so-called "grand-daddy" of all college football bowls. In 1936, Fordham, too, had sought a Rose Bowl bid prior to its 7−7 tie with Georgia in late November. The Rams' dreams of roses eventually went unfulfilled, and so did their hope for any bowl, for that matter.

Junior Frank Sinkwich had followed an excellent sophomore season with outstanding play through the first three games of 1941. "Fireball Frankie" was aspiring to become only Georgia's third All-American halfback in its history, despite breaking his jaw against South Carolina in the second game of the year. Prior to the Columbia game a couple of wires had been removed from Sinkwich's healing jaw. He could open his jaw about half an inch and, according to Butts, had progressed to eating eggs.

Regarded as the best player at Georgia since Vernon "Catfish" Smith (1929–1931), Sinkwich was determined to be named All-American by season's end and knew playing well in New York could help his cause. He told Georgia football's publicist prior to the game, "I want you to get me in every paper in New York before the Columbia game next Saturday. If I don't make all the papers after the game, that's my fault." The press portrayed the game as the "Fireball" versus Columbia's star back, Paul Governali—a future All-American in his own right.

In front of 27,000 fans, the Bulldogs forced the host to punt on the opening drive. Georgia took over on Columbia's 45-yard line and eventually faced third-and-7 from the Lions' 10-yard line. Sinkwich dropped back, apparently to pass, but instead took off, running around right tackle to score a touchdown. Columbia tallied a field goal in the opening quarter, but the game remained scoreless thereafter. Georgia defeated the nationally ranked Lions 7–3. Columbia's offense and the acclaimed Governali gained only 134 total yards for the contest, including just three yards rushing.

Don't Look Up!

Georgia football has had its long line of successful place-kickers over the last three decades, namely Allan Leavitt (1973–1976), Rex Robinson (1977–1980), Kevin Butler (1981–1984), John Kasay (1987–1990), Billy Bennett (2000–2003), and presently Brandon Coutu (2004–2006). However, it can be said that the Bulldogs' initial accomplished kicker was kicking extra points nearly 70 years ago—Leo Costa (1940–1942).

Costa was credited with playing very little in competition at Georgia because game time was suspended during an extra point attempt. He did earn a few minutes of playing time as a substitute in Georgia's starting lineup once or twice. Costa never attempted a field goal. In fact, since 1933, when the SEC first began keeping records, the Bulldogs made just one field goal in their first 20 seasons in the conference (1933–1952) when Frank Sinkwich kicked against Florida in 1941. At a time when a point-after attempt was far from a certainty in college football, Costa was as accurate as they were in the sport.

In his three years on Georgia's varsity, Costa converted 83 percent of his point-after attempts. In contrast, all of college football in 1940 was successful on 61 percent of its tries. Costa's accomplishments include his senior season of 1942, when he ranked seventh in the SEC in scoring with 43 points (43 of 54 on points after). After 64 seasons, his 43 successful points after still rank fourth of all time at Georgia for a single season. Although Costa is barely credited with playing in a game, his successful points after were the difference in three Georgia victories during his career: 1940 versus Auburn (14–13), 1940 versus Georgia Tech (21–19), and 1942 against Kentucky (7–6).

Costa would never look up from the ground when kicking the

ball. Instead, he would keep his head down after each kick, lean over, and pretend to pick up an imaginary half dollar off the grass. His holder during the 1941 and 1942 seasons, Davis, would inform Costa if his attempt was successful or not. Once during practice Costa looked up after a kick. Outraged, line coach Whitworth made the kicker run around the track for three hours.

Going Bowling for the First Time

Through nearly five decades of excellence entering the 1941 season, Georgia had not once participated in a postseason bowl game. The Bulldogs had come close on a few occasions but remained one of just four conference teams in the 12-member SEC not to have played in a bowl. In fact, eight SEC teams had played in a combined 21 bowls in their histories (eight Rose, six Sugar, six Orange, and one Bacardi Bowl) before the Bulldogs finally earned a trip to Miami's Orange Bowl, capping the 1941 season.

The Bulldogs' season was highlighted with wins over Columbia, Dartmouth, Georgia Tech, and Auburn on what would now be distinguished as a Hail Mary pass play. Georgia and Auburn were scoreless when, with three seconds left in the game, the Bulldogs had the ball on their own 35. Sinkwich heaved a pass 40 yards downfield to Davis. The Racehorse caught the ball on Auburn's 25-yard line and sprinted the rest of the way with no time remaining for a miraculous Georgia victory.

It appeared that Ole Miss, which had tied Georgia 14–14 in October, was heading to the Orange Bowl when it was upset by Mississippi State 21–0. The Rebels were out of contention, and the Bulldogs got invited to Miami for a January 1 matchup with the Southwest Conference runner-up, Texas Christian University.

Similar to Alabama, Tennessee, Louisiana State University, and Tulane of the SEC, Texas Christian was familiar with making postseason plans, but it was the first team ever from the SWC to play in the Orange Bowl. The Horned Frogs had been to four bowls in their history, including three in a four-season span

(1935–1938) under their coach at the time, Leo "Dutch" Mayer. Texas Christian's trio of distinguished passers, Kyle Gillespie, Emery Nix, and Dean Bagley, was one of the better passing offenses in the nation, throwing for 1,149 yards during the year. Gillespie was to Texas Christian as Sinkwich was to Georgia. Gillespie was a triple threat with the ability to run, pass, and punt, and also called the offense's plays.

The Bulldogs arrived in Miami on December 26 after leaving the Central of Georgia depot on Christmas Day. Georgia brought its entire squad of 45 players, more than any of the other nine bowl teams that season, and included injured captain Heyward Allen (broken arm) and fullback Dick McPhee (recovering from an appendectomy). Although Georgia had never sent a player to a bowl game, one Bulldog had actually played in the Orange Bowl before. Junior lineman Gene Ellenson was from Miami and had played as a high schooler in Burdine Stadium, site of the Orange Bowl.

The Bulldogs were able to escape for some entertainment while in the city of Miami. A few days before the game, the team visited the Miami Biltmore Water Follies. To honor the Bulldogs, a band mistakenly began to play what it thought was Georgia's fight song—Georgia Tech's "Rambling Wreck." Several players quickly stopped the music. Later, the band conductor left to work another gig for a cocktail hour. As he was leaving, a Georgia player, joking about the band's mishap, shouted to the conductor: "Don't let that happen again, Toscanini." (Arturo Toscanini was an Italian musician considered by many as the greatest conductor in the world during the first half of the 20th century.)

Also before the game, a Miami dog track asked for permission from Georgia officials to have a "Frank Sinkwich Night" at the track. Georgia administrators acknowledged that a "Georgia Night" could be a possibility, but they opposed that the night be dedicated to a single player. The track was upset at first but later relented and honored the entire Georgia team.

Georgia opened its first few practices in Miami to writers and photographers. However, on December 29, Coach Wally Butts closed the team off to outsiders, and the Bulldogs held secret practice sessions. Any fun the players would have would come after the bowl game. It would have to be mostly business, not pleasure, prior to the first postseason appearance in the school's history.

Getting Down to Business

The 35,786 spectators who witnessed the 1942 Orange Bowl between Georgia and Texas Christian comprised the largest attendance in the first 12 years of the bowl. The contest's pregame pageantry was described as the most colorful and attractive of any previous bowl. During warm-ups, the players ran through strings of oranges onto the field while nearly 20 different bands later played in unison. When Texas Christian entered the field, a man dressed as a cowboy fired his pistols in the air. Seemingly, the only event that did not receive any kind of fanfare was when Georgia ran on to the field for the start of the game.

The Bulldogs defeated Texas Christian 40–26 in one of the finest bowl performances in college football history by a single player. Georgia's Sinkwich was spectacular, throwing for 243 yards and three touchdowns on nine of 13 passes. He rushed for 139 yards and a score. With six minutes remaining in the opening quarter, the Horned Frogs led 7–6, only to see Georgia score 27 consecutive points en route to a 33–7 halftime lead. In the second half, Fireball Frankie ran for a 43-yard touchdown and, following Costa's point after, Georgia led 40–7.

Unlike before, Texas Christian suddenly began moving the ball with ease against the Bulldogs in the third quarter. Georgia seemed particularly defenseless at one of the guard positions. Coach Butts, who had earlier replaced guard Harry Kuniansky with a substitute, called for Kuniansky to return to the ballgame. Line coach Whitworth looked everywhere on the sideline and the bench for Kuniansky, but he was nowhere to be found. Finally, Whitworth spotted him standing against a concrete structure that supported a section of stands. Kuniansky was eating an orange, and his headgear was also half-filled with the fruit. The oranges he collected had been strung across the players' tunnel and also arranged as yard-line markers.

"Come here!" boomed Whitworth. Surprised and frightened, Kuniansky dropped his orange and quickly crammed his headgear onto his head. He had forgotten about the oranges he had placed inside his headgear, and orange juice ran down his face as he frantically dashed back into action.

In the highest-scoring bowl game until 1945, Georgia allowed three second-half scores but eventually was victorious. Both teams stayed in Miami two additional days following the game and returned home on January 4.

The Bulldogs celebrated their victory by fishing and visiting a horse track. At the Tropical Park track, several players bet on a horse named War Declared on a hunch. They had decided to wager on this particular horse after observing the owner's name, A. Sinkenich, similar to Sinkwich. There was no way War Declared could lose! However, much to the dismay of the wagering Bulldogs, the performance of War Declared in the race was not quite as sensational as Sinkwich's play in the game. The horse finished in third place.

chapter 7

Two Championships with Charley

Coach Wally Butts hands the ball off to Charley Trippi in practice before the January 1, 1943, Rose Bowl game against UCLA in Pasadena, California. Standing left to right behind them are Frank Plant, Ardie McClure, Walter Ruark, and Ken Keuper.

Winning the Heisman before the Hype

Led by Sinkwich, the greatest player in college football, Georgia cruised through its first nine games of the 1942 season, defeating the opposition by an average of more than 30 points per victory. However, the number one–ranked Bulldogs were upset by Auburn on November 21, losing their first game since late October 1941.

Things were not any easier for Georgia the following week when it hosted Georgia Tech, the second-ranked team in the nation. It was the last game for 13 seniors in Sanford Stadium, including Sinkwich. After playing halfback his entire career, Sinkwich was starting his third-consecutive game at fullback to allow sophomore halfback Charley Trippi into the starting lineup. In pregame warm-ups, Sinkwich wore an *S* on his back, not for Superman but for his initiation into the Sphinx Club—the highest honor for a student on the University of Georgia campus.

Sinkwich rushed for 72 yards, passed for 92 more, and intercepted a pass on defense in an easy 34–0 victory by the Bulldogs. Trippi was even more impressive, tossing two touchdowns and rushing for 114 yards on 11 carries, including an 87-yard scoring run. After the win, Coach Butts walked into Georgia's jubilant locker room. As he raised his hand to speak, celebrating players surrounded him and dragged him under a freezing-cold shower. All Coach Butts could do was grin and bear the frigid water.

Also following the game, Sinkwich received a telegram stating he had been selected Player of the Year in college football and would receive the eighth annual Heisman Memorial Trophy. About the same time, Georgia football's publicist told the stadium's press box that Sinkwich had won the Heisman. Georgia fan Billy Hooper overheard the announcement and declared, "Well, that's the oddest thing I ever heard. You boys probably don't know how odd it is, a Georgia man winning a Tech trophy." John Heisman, after whom the trophy is named, was once the athletic director of the Downtown Athletic Club of New York, where the trophy is still presented today. Prior to serving in that position, Heisman won

170 games in 35 seasons as head coach at six institutions. Most notably, he coached at Georgia Tech from 1904 through 1919, where he achieved a record of 102–29–7.

On December 8, 1942, Sinkwich, accompanied by Butts, received the Heisman Trophy at a dinner attended by 850 guests at the Downtown Athletic Club. Because he was a member of the U.S. Marine Reserves during World War II, Sinkwich accepted the trophy wearing his private first class Marine Corps uniform. The dinner also honored Columbia's Paul Governali, who finished second in the Heisman voting and also wore a military uniform. A total of 841 points separated first and second place in the voting, representing the widest margin in Heisman voting until 1951.

In the last decade or so, the presentation of college football's Heisman Trophy has become a colossal and highly publicized event. The recipient is not announced prior to the Heisman Trophy ceremony, the winner gives an acceptance speech, and television runs the *Heisman Trophy Presentation Presented by (insert sponsor here)* before a national prime-time audience. When Frank Sinkwich received the award in 1942, the votes had been counted prior to his last regular season game, there was no media hype, there was no recipient speech, and the winner had already been announced 10 days beforehand.

California, Here I Come

Georgia finished the 1942 regular season with its first 10-win campaign in history and a number-two national ranking. The Bulldogs were rewarded with a trip to Pasadena, California, to face Pac-10 champion UCLA on January 1, 1943.

Several days leading up to the game, the team met a number of Hollywood stars, including Rita Hayworth, Bob Hope, Pat O'Brien, and Ginger Rogers. Frank Freeman, an executive at Paramount Studios, invited the Bulldogs to a "movie star luncheon." Freeman was from Atlanta and a Georgia Tech graduate, but that was not held against him. The team, Coach Butts and his wife, and other Georgia officials and boosters gladly attended the luncheon.

Frank Sinkwich (center) is besieged by autograph seekers at a dinner in New York City, where he was awarded the Heisman Trophy on December 8, 1942.

Music played in the banquet room and at some point during the reception, Georgia Tech's "Rambling Wreck" was jokingly blared by Freeman. Georgia had participated in only two bowl games to that point in its history, and, on both occasions, the Bulldogs had to endure the playing of their in-state rival's fight song.

Despite Georgia's ability to move the ball easily on UCLA while holding the Bruins' offense at bay, the two teams were surprisingly scoreless through three quarters. On the first play of the final quarter, Georgia's Red Boyd blocked a punt that went out of the end zone for a Bulldog safety. Midway in the fourth quarter,

Sinkwich was inserted back into the game despite having two injured ankles. He scored on a two-yard run on fourth down to cap a remarkable career at Georgia. Although Sinkwich was limited to 33 yards on 11 carries in the 9–0 victory, sophomore Trippi picked up the slack by rushing for 115 yards on 27 carries.

Unfortunately, the Bulldogs would be without both star half-backs the following '43 season. Sinkwich went to the NFL's Detroit Lions, and Trippi entered the U.S. Air Force.

Along with Sinkwich and end George Poschner, guard Walter Ruark was one of three Bulldogs to be named first-team All-SEC in 1942. Ruark is a remarkable story, according to Coach Butts. He just showed up on campus one day and asked for a football uniform. He turned out to be a two-time all-conference player and one of the best guards in the school's history.

Ruark later made the ultimate sacrifice when he was killed in World War II when fighting in Europe. The University of Georgia football had lost five players in World War I and tragically would lose 10 more in World War II. Besides Ruark, those men were end John Brown, guard Will Burt, guard Winfred Goodman, guard Winston Hodgson, guard Howard "Smiley" Johnson, guard Red Maddox, center Homer Passmore, end James Skipworth, and center Tom Witt.

Against All Odds

With the start of the 1943 season, the personnel demand of World War II had carried off many of college football's players into the draft. Only four of the 12 SEC schools fielded teams in '43, with those universities located in the two states of Georgia and Louisiana: Georgia, Georgia Tech, LSU, and Tulane. Georgia was especially thin because not only did some Bulldogs join the military, but many key players were lost to graduation and some were injured in the preseason. As Georgia neared the start of the season, Coach Butts's lineup had no starters from the season before and featured all 17-year-old freshmen with the exception of junior tackle Mike Castronis.

The depletion of players was compounded further when the U.S. Army decided that six more players in advanced ROTC would also not be allowed to play. That could have been the straw that broke the Bulldog's back. Coach Butts now came to the realization there was little hope of winning more than one or two games during the year.

One day prior to Georgia's season opener against Presbyterian College, Butts decided to ask his team if they wanted to join most of the SEC and cancel football for the season. If the players agreed to do so, Georgia's schedule would be eliminated immediately. "I asked them frankly if they wanted to pay the price in defeats they'll have to take," said Butts. Georgia players agreed to do so. "So we'll play football as long as 11 men are available to put a team on the field," said Butts. He and his Bulldogs would not join the majority of the conference, which appeared to place the possibility of a poor win-loss record above everything else. Instead, the decision was made by the Georgia team to honor the games that had been scheduled.

Presbyterian's experienced team, filled with seniors, had pummeled Fort Jackson the week before 41–0 and was a heavy favorite over the Bulldogs. The Bulldogs not only shocked Presbyterian 25–7, but the victory stunned most of the college football world. In front of only 6,000 spectators at Sanford Stadium, Georgia intercepted nine Blue Hose passes, which still remains tied for an SEC single-game record. Most importantly, it discovered a new set of "touchdown twins" in freshmen Johnny Cook and Charles "Rabbit" Smith, replacing Sinkwich and Trippi. The Bulldogs lost a heartbreaker the following week in the last minute of play against LSU, the eventual Orange Bowl champion. The setback was followed with victories over Tennessee Tech and Wake Forest by a combined score of 74–0. Georgia, presumed to experience its "most dismal gridiron campaign" in its history, was instead 3–1 and ranked 20th in the nation.

The Bulldogs lost their next game to Daniel Field, which was not an individual player or person, but a team of former college stars, in Augusta, Georgia. Next, LSU defeated Georgia for a second time, but the Bulldogs rebounded to win their next three contests.

Inexperienced, young, and withstanding an ever-changing starting lineup, Georgia was 6–3 and held a scoring margin of nearly 18 points per game.

Unlike Georgia but resembling some college teams at the time, Georgia Tech's football squad was made up of Navy V-12 and other military trainees. The military Yellow Jackets hammered the amateur Bulldogs 48–0 in the season finale. In the following season of 1944, the circumstances were the same as the previous year for both state schools. Georgia consisted primarily of freshmen too young for the war's draft or players who could not meet the military's physical standards. Georgia Tech, on the other hand, was again made up of predominantly military trainees. The result of the game between the schools was also similar in '44, as the Yellow Jackets soundly defeated the Bulldogs 44–0. In chronicling the series results between the Bulldogs and the Jackets, Georgia discredits the two Yellow Jacket victories in 1943 and 1944. However, Georgia Tech considers its two victories valid despite having fielded a squad supplemented by the V-12 Navy College Training Program. Including the two crushing losses to Georgia Tech in 1943 and 1944, Georgia still achieved a creditable 13–7 combined record for the two seasons.

Praise for Poschner

End George Poschner, a member of Georgia's "Fabulous Frosh of '39," was an excellent receiver and just as exceptional on the defensive side of the ball. Poschner was selected first-team All-American in 1942, but his actions off the field were even more honorable.

Both Poschner and his childhood friend, halfback Sinkwich, grew up in Youngstown, Ohio. Following high school, Sinkwich accepted a football scholarship from Georgia on the condition that Poschner also would be given one. Following his brilliant career in Athens, Poschner was one of several Bulldogs to serve in World War II.

On January 8, 1945, Lieutenant Poschner was engaged in the Battle of the Bulge—a 41-day attempt by Germany to split the British and the American line of forces. During the conflict, Poschner was severely injured by machine-gun fire and lay wounded in a frozen Belgian field for four days. As a consequence of his injuries, he lost both legs and part of a hand.

While he recuperated, the Poschner Fund was established to assist in the payment of expenses. On October 11, 1945, Jim W. Woodruff Jr., a well-known radio and later television personality in Columbus, Georgia, broadcasted the Poschner Fund on Armed Forces Radio. While overseas, Woodruff contributed the only U.S. currency ($20) he had in his pocket at the time to the fund. "All of us remember his [Poschner's] exploits and 'will-to-win' spirit on the gridiron," Woodruff announced. "He carried that spirit with him when he went to the battlefields of Europe."

Poschner was also shot in the head during the battle and had to have two plates implanted. He once said with a grin, "Yeah, I've got two plates in my head, but thank goodness I still have my own teeth." Poschner would receive the Purple Heart, Bronze Star Medal, and Distinguished Service Cross for his bravery and gallantry during the war. In 1982, he was inducted into the Georgia Sports Hall of Fame. In that same year at a testimonial dinner, Sinkwich said of his childhood friend and ex-teammate, "Knowing George has made me stronger all my life."

Charley's Homecoming

As World War II ended in 1945, college football teams were hardly supplemented by the military. Georgia began the season with a record of 4–0, and the Bulldogs' outlook appeared even more promising when it was announced that Trippi would be rejoining the team.

Trippi was the 1943 Rose Bowl's most outstanding player as a sophomore after gaining 1,239 yards of total offense during the '42 regular season. Sergeant Trippi spent nearly the next three

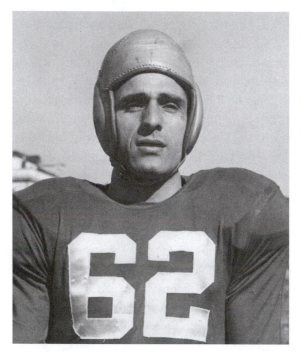

Charley Trippi returned to finish school at Georgia after the war, and it was no coincidence that he helped to lift the Bulldogs to dominance.

years in the Air Force, starring on the Third Air Force's football team. On October 13, 1945, the U.S. war department released Trippi by request of Georgia's Senator Richard B. Russell on a "surplus and hardship" basis.

The 12th-ranked and undefeated Bulldogs, including Trippi, hosted LSU on October 20. Trippi was a marked man the entire game and managed just 29 of Georgia's 30 yards on the ground. He also had a 40-yard punting average, but the Bulldogs were devastated 32–0. The following week, Georgia played in Birmingham, Alabama, against number-six Alabama, the eventual winner of the SEC and Rose Bowl. Down 7–0 in the opening quarter, Trippi made a 31-yard scoring run that was, according to the *Constitution*, "one of the most sensational touchdown runs ever seen on Legion Field." The Bulldogs would eventually lose 28–14, but no team played as well against the Crimson Tide that year.

Georgia was unexpectedly 0–2 since Trippi's return but promptly went on one of the most spectacular winning stretches in the school's history. The Bulldogs closed out the season with five consecutive victories, outscoring their opponents 156–13. Trippi was just as amazing as his fellow Dogs. His 239 rushing yards against Florida and 323 passing and 384 total offensive yards versus Georgia Tech were all SEC single-game records for many years. In the Oil Bowl against Tulsa, Trippi threw a 65-yard score and returned a punt for a 68-yard touchdown in a 20–6 Georgia win. This winning streak was a sign of things to come for Trippi and the Bulldogs in 1946.

Pennsylvanian Homesick Blues

John Rauch is one of the greatest quarterbacks in Bulldog football history. His 36 wins as a starting quarterback at Georgia, from 1945 to 1948, were an NCAA record for 30 years, until Michigan's Rick Leach won 38 from 1975 to 1978. Rauch's celebrated and extraordinary career at Georgia almost did not unfold.

As the story is told by Trippi, Rauch became seriously homesick when he was a freshman at Georgia in 1945. Without notifying his coaches, he decided he would board a train and return home to Pennsylvania. On his way to the train station and with suitcase in hand, Rauch just happen to bump into one of Georgia's assistant coaches. The coach asked where the quarterback was going. "I'm taking my laundry," Rauch guiltily replied. The coach knew better and discussed the pros and cons of his leaving Georgia, emphasizing the latter. The freshman signal caller changed his mind and decided to remain at Georgia.

John Rauch would become a three-time all-conference selection and a 1948 first-team All-American. His 4,044 career passing yards were an all-time NCAA record until 1950. Following a three-year stint in pro football, Rauch coached on the collegiate and professional levels for 25 years. He is one of only 11 former Georgia players inducted into the College Football Hall of Fame, an induction that likely would not have occurred if Rauch, on his way home to Pennsylvania, had not happened upon an assistant coach.

An Unsung Bulldog

Led by tailback Trippi, guard Herb St. John, quarterback John Rauch, and end Joe Tereshinski, Georgia eased through the 1946 season. The Bulldogs achieved a perfect 11–0 record, defeating all of their opponents by at least 10 points. Although Georgia was selected first in the nation by the Williamson poll, either Army or Notre Dame, who had each suffered a tie, was chosen as national champion by every other poll.

An unsung star on Georgia's '46 squad was tackle Garland "Bulldog" Williams. Because of the interruption of World War II during the 1943–1944 seasons, several Bulldogs saw significant playing time on the team of '42 and then again four seasons later in '46. Only Williams started at least eight games in each of the championship seasons.

According to writer Jack Troy, Williams "didn't have the faintest idea about a defense or offense's plan." Georgia was working on defense one day in practice when Williams, according to Troy, "ignored his assignment…if he realized he had any special one." Coach Butts called to him, "Bulldog, where were you on that play?" Williams curiously answered, "Coach, I was back there and amongst 'em."

Rauch's Coming-Out

After narrowly defeating Furman 13–7 in the 1947 season opener, the Bulldogs were beaten by North Carolina on a last-minute touchdown pass. The loss to the Tar Heels snapped a 17-game winning streak, which today still remains a school record.

Things were not looking any better the following week for Georgia when it hosted LSU on October 4. The Bulldogs had never defeated the Tigers, losing the first seven games of the series by an average of more than 17 points per defeat. LSU had finished eighth in the nation the previous year and began the '47 season with a win over a good Rice University team. The Tigers returned most of their starters from '46, including quarterback Y.A.

Tittle, one of the nation's best passers and, eventually, one of the NFL's greatest players. Georgia was inexperienced and had lost standouts end Tereshinski, tackle Williams, fullback Dick McPhee, and one of the very best Bulldogs of all time, back Trippi, from the year before. It was believed that Georgia would do well in losing to the Tigers by "only" 14 points.

The game began as expected. LSU scored two quick touchdowns on a Tittle pass following a Bulldog fumble and an interception return. However, Georgia unexpectedly led 14–12 at halftime following a Floyd Reid touchdown run and a Rauch scoring pass to Dan Edwards. In the third quarter, the Tigers would regain the lead 19–14, but the Bulldogs would score three unanswered touchdowns to eventually win 35–19.

Tittle and the rest of the Tiger offense could only accumulate 102 yards of total offense. Georgia's balanced ground game featured 56 yards from Reid, 55 by John Donaldson, 52 from Stan Nestorak, and 42 yards by Billy Henderson. Nevertheless, the Bulldogs' primary offensive weapon was quarterback Rauch. Junior Rauch, overshadowed by Trippi as a freshman and as a sophomore, completed 12 of 18 passes for 143 yards and three scores. The *Journal* wrote the next day, "Johnny Rauch, the man who found himself, and directed one of the most exciting victories Sanford Field ever produced."

No Ordinary Joe

Georgia was 4–1 and ranked 18th in the Associated Press poll when it met Alabama in Birmingham on October 30, 1948. The Crimson Tide, 2–2–1 after five games, was off to its worst start since 1922, but a victory over Mississippi State the week before had apparently jump-started 'Bama's season. The Bulldogs were seven-point favorites at newly enlarged Legion Field in front of the largest crowd ever to see a football game in the state.

Georgia got its revenge after losing to the Crimson Tide by 10 points the year before in Athens, dismantling Alabama by a score of 35–0. It was the Crimson Tide's worst loss in 38 years in what remains the most lopsided win by the Bulldogs in the series. Alabama completed just two of 13 passes for 37 yards and was intercepted six times. Half of those interceptions were corralled by Joe Jackura, a little-known center who played the game of his life.

Jackura, according to the *Constitution*, was "an unheralded center, who before Saturday [the Alabama game] was really just another guy called Joe." He intercepted three Alabama passes in Georgia's decisive victory. One of his three picks was returned for a score when he intercepted Bob Cochran at his own 20-yard line and, aided by a key block from Weyman Sellers at midfield, dashed 80 yards for a touchdown. What makes Jackura's defensive feat so astounding is that in two and a half years at Georgia prior to the Alabama game, Jackura had not intercepted a single pass, nor would he corral any additional opponents' passes the rest of the '48 season. Jackura's three interceptions in a single game share a school record with Jeff Hipp (1979 versus Georgia Tech), Terry Hoage (1982 versus Vanderbilt), and Tra Battle (2006 versus Auburn).

chapter 8
A Decade of Ups but Mostly Downs

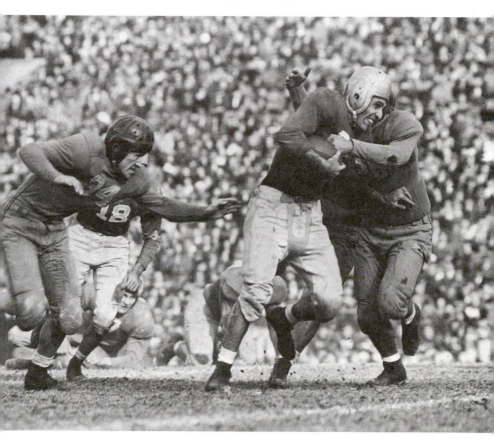

While Charley Trippi, shown in the 1945 game against Georgia Tech in Atlanta, and the rest of the Bulldogs were dominant in the 1940s, much of the 1950s would have more misses than hits for Georgia football.

A Victory Nap

Following Georgia's successful stretch from 1941 to 1948, when it won nearly 80 percent of its games and participated in six bowls, the Bulldogs endured a 4–6–1 campaign in '49—Georgia's first losing season in 10 years. The outlook for the 1950 season was less than optimistic, and the Bulldogs were not scheduled to open with a "patsy" as in years past. The season opener was not going to be against Furman, Chattanooga, Citadel, or the like.

Georgia hosted mighty Maryland to begin the year, a rematch of the 1948 Gator Bowl that ended in a 20–20 tie. While the Bulldogs were coming off a subpar season, the Terrapins had finished 9–1 in '49 and were victorious in the Gator Bowl. Georgia's roster was filled with inexperienced sophomores, whereas number-15 Maryland featured three preseason All-Americans: tackle Ray Krouse, guard Bob Ward, and end Elmer Wingate.

On a sweltering September 23 in Athens, Georgia capitalized on five Maryland fumbles to upset the Terrapins 27–7. A band of Bulldog sophomores, backs Zippy Morocco, Fred Bilyeu, and Lauren Hargrove, linebacker Derwent Langley, and guard Frank Salerno, led Georgia in the impressive victory.

When the contest was over, Coach Butts was hoisted onto the shoulders of his players and carried to midfield to meet Maryland coach Jim Tatum. After shaking hands, Butts was raised again and carried toward a stadium gate leading out of the playing field. Once Butts was let down under one of the crossbars, he walked over to the hedges bordering the field and inexplicably laid down and sprawled out on the grass.

A photographer approached the resting Butts and asked if he could take his photo. Butts raised himself on one elbow and asked, "How do you want me?" "Just like you are will be fine," answered the photographer. Butts, exhausted from the tension generated by the game and the intense heat, fell back onto the grass.

Following the win over Maryland, it would be more than nine years before Georgia would defeat a ranked opponent, having a dismal 0–20–2 record against ranked opposition during that span of time. After a 6–3–3 record in 1950, the Bulldogs would have only two winning seasons over the next eight years. For most of the decade of the 1950s, Georgia football enjoyed few successful seasons but several notable victories and events.

"The Brat" Passes the Babe

Edmund Raymond "Zeke" Bratkowski from Danville, Illinois, followed Frank Sinkwich, Johnny Cook, and John Rauch as the next gifted and conference-leading quarterback for the Bulldogs. In each of his three seasons at Georgia, Bratkowski finished no lower than seventh in the nation in passing. He was selected first-team All-American in his junior and senior seasons of 1952 and 1953. Although the Bulldogs slumped to a 15–17 record during Bratkowski's three years, "the Brat" led several celebrated victories, most notably a win over Miami on a Friday night in December.

In 1952, Bratkowski's best season at Georgia, the Bulldogs, sporting a 6–4 record, played Miami in the last game of the season. Georgia had accomplished its winning record against a rigorous schedule, and some in the media felt Coach Butts should receive Coach of the Year recognition in the conference. Bratkowski entered the game 117 passing yards short of the SEC's single-season record. Kentucky's Babe Parilli had passed for 1,643 yards the season before to set the conference mark.

Without Harry Babcock, Bratkowski's and the SEC's leading receiver, Harry Babock, Bratkowski broke Parilli's record before the first half was completed. For the game, Bratkowski completed 16 of 23 passes for 297 yards with touchdown passes to Bob Dellinger, Johnny Carson, and Art DeCarlo in a 35–13 Georgia win. As Bratkowski's two main receivers, Carson caught seven passes for 160 yards and DeCarlo had 108 receiving yards on six receptions. The following day, the *Journal* opened its coverage of the game with, "The Zeke Bratkwoski aerial circus invaded Orange Bowl Stadium Friday night, and 21,597 screaming football fans and the University of Miami grid team went away shaking their heads and asking, 'Who is Babe Parilli?'"

A 3–8 campaign in 1953 was Georgia's worst since 1905. The eight losses remain the most in the school's 113-season history. One of the few bright spots during the season was the play of Bratkowski. In a game against Mississippi Southern College (now known as University of Southern Mississippi) on November 21, it was later researched and calculated that Bratkowski broke the NCAA record for most passing yards in a career. John Ford of Hardin-Simmons had set the record of 4,736 passing yards in 1950, breaking Rauch's mark of 4,004 yards.

Playing in his next-to-last collegiate game, Bratkowski completed a 15-yard pass to freshman Harold Pilgrim late in the game of a 14–0 Georgia loss. Bratkowski's completion passed Ford's mark and added to a number of records Bratkowski established during his time at Georgia. In addition to having an accurate arm, Bratkowski was also an excellent punter and led the nation with a punting average of 42.6 in 1953. Despite the Bulldogs' poor record that season, Bratkowski was named first-team All-American by *Focus* magazine and, along with teammate Carson, a third-team All-American by the United Press.

Bratkowski enjoyed a 14-year NFL career with Chicago, Los Angeles, and Green Bay. He was a member of Green Bay's Super Bowl champion teams of 1966 and 1967, serving as the backup quarterback to Hall of Famer Bart Starr. Bratkowski followed his playing days in the NFL with an extensive coaching career in the league. The Brat's NCAA record of 4,863 career passing yards has long been surpassed, but it stills remains fifth best of all time at Georgia.

Wide Right!

After the disastrous 1953 season and the loss of quarterback Bratkowski, the Bulldogs opened 1954 winning three of its first four games. Their only loss was to Texas A&M, the Aggie team on which Jim Dent's book and the movie *The Junction Boys* are based.

On October 16, Georgia opened conference play against Vanderbilt for homecoming. The Bulldogs were six-point favorites, despite missing regulars Roy Wilkins, John Bell, and Donald Shea. Georgia scored touchdowns on a 15-yard pass from Dick Young to Charlie Madison and a 59-run by Bobby Garrard, who finished the game with 112 rushing yards on 12 carries. Nevertheless, Vanderbilt held a 14–13 lead late in the contest.

With only minutes remaining in the game, Georgia captain Joe O'Malley blocked a Commodore punt that was recovered by Willie Fowler on Vanderbilt's 25-yard line. The Bulldogs' offense moved the ball a little downfield and on fourth down called upon Joe Graff to attempt a 24-yard field goal with approximately three minutes remaining.

Graff, normally a left guard, had never kicked a field goal during his collegiate career. In fact, he had made only one of three extra-point attempts for Georgia in 1953. As mentioned earlier, a field-goal attempt was a rare occurrence in college football during this time. In 1954, only 48 field goals were successfully kicked in all of college football, compared to 1,525 in 2005. Up until Graff's attempt, one could likely count on two hands how many success-ful field goals Georgia had made in its history. Prior to Sam Mrvos kicking one against Tulane in 1953, the previous successful field goal had been kicked by Sinkwich 12 years prior. Albeit only a 24-yard attempt, the odds were certainly not in Graff's favor. Regardless, his kick was good, and the Bulldogs jumped to a 16–14 lead.

In the final minutes, Vanderbilt mounted a drive, and their kicker Bobby Goodall was called upon to attempt a game-winning kick. For the year, Goodall had been perfect on one field goal and seven point-after attempts but would miss wide right against Georgia with fewer than 10 seconds remaining in the contest.

The Bulldogs' record improved to 4–1, surpassing its victory total for the entire previous season. By mid-November, Georgia shockingly stood at 6–1–1 and was ranked 20th in the nation. However, the Bulldogs would lose their final two games to Auburn and Georgia Tech by a combined score of 42–3. What was Georgia's only score in its final two contests of 1954? A 26-yard field goal by Graff against Georgia Tech—the first field goal by the Bulldogs in their 61-year series with the Yellow Jackets.

Another Comeback against the Commodores

To begin the 1955 season, Georgia faced Ole Miss at Atlanta's Grant Field in the second game of a doubleheader, which featured Georgia Tech and Miami in the first game. The Bulldogs were defeated 26–13 by a Rebel team that would eventually win the Cotton Bowl and finish with a 10–1 record.

On September 24, Georgia hosted Vanderbilt in Athens for the second consecutive season. The Commodores were an excellent team, led by halfback Charley Horton who, to date, is one of only 33 Vanderbilt football players ever to receive any type of All-American recognition.

On the day of the game, former Georgia coach (1910–1919) and Vanderbilt player (1906) Alex Cunningham led a pep rally at the university's Stegeman Hall. Artie Pew, a Georgia player under Cunningham, joined in the rally recalling memorable incidents of the Georgia-Vanderbilt football series. Assistant coach Bill Hartman gave a scouting report on the Commodores, while assistant Spec Landrum introduced 50 freshman Bullpup players to the crowd.

Vanderbilt led 13–0 early in the final quarter of the game following a Horton scoring rush and a Don Orr touchdown pass. Commodore kicker Tommy Woodroof missed the second point-after attempt. Georgia's Dick Young, a backup quarterback the previous year and at the start of the '55 season, came off the bench to hopefully ignite a sputtering Bulldog offense. Young led Georgia on a 56-yard drive capped by an 11-yard touchdown pass to Cleve Clark with 13:25 remaining in the game. Ron Cooper's point after was successful, and the Bulldogs had reduced their deficit to six points. With fewer than four minutes remaining in the contest, Young scored on a two-yard run following a 27-yard pass to Jimmy Orr. Joe Comfort's successful point-after attempt gave Georgia a slim 14–13 lead.

Vanderbilt threw four consecutive incomplete passes on its final drive, and the Bulldogs took over on downs. Georgia ran out the clock and recorded its second-straight victory over the Commodores in comeback fashion. Young, who completed nine of 17 passes for 139 yards, had entered the game by first throwing long, incomplete tosses but then shortened his throws to lead the Georgia rally. After the win, Coach Butts remarked, "Young played his best game for us today.... He gave me anxious moments when he [threw] those long ones, though."

Although the Bulldogs would finish the '55 campaign with a losing 4–6 record, the season was highlighted with their resurgent victory over the skilled Commodores. Vanderbilt ended the year with an 8–3 record, including a win over Auburn in the Gator Bowl—still the only bowl victory in the school's history.

The Drought-Breaker

As Georgia prepared for the 1957 season finale, the Bulldogs were assuredly headed for eight losses in a season (for the second time in five years) and their worst campaign in 52 seasons. Georgia had won only two of nine games and had scored a total of 13 touchdowns for the season, with five of those coming against a winless Kentucky squad in late October. As Georgia's downward spiral had begun with the 1949 season, so did its losing skid against its final opponent of '57, Georgia Tech. The Bulldogs had dropped eight consecutive games against the Yellow Jackets, averaging slightly more than a 17-point deficit per defeat.

Georgia Tech was experiencing an unusually poor season. After averaging close to a 10–1 record the previous six years, the Yellow Jackets were 4–3–2 and would not receive a bowl invitation for the first time since 1950. Although the Bulldogs' record was unimpressive, they had barely lost to Auburn in their previous game by a 6–0 score. The Tigers would finish the year undefeated, untied, and the Associated Press's national champion. Notwithstanding, Georgia Tech was a 6½-point favorite over Georgia in a series where pregame odds mattered very little.

In front of a sell-out crowd of 40,000 at Grant Field, with a 35-degree temperature accompanied by a stiff wind, Georgia and Georgia Tech battled to a scoreless tie at halftime. On the first series of the second half, Georgia Tech drove 38 yards from its own 15-yard line. Reaching Georgia's side of the field, Claude Faucette fumbled, and Georgia's Theron Sapp recovered on the 50-yard line.

After netting just 11 yards on five consecutive runs, the Bulldogs faced third-and-12 on Tech's 39-yard line. Quarterback Charley Britt completed Georgia's only pass of the day for 13 yards to Jimmy Orr: Orr eventually became known as one of the best receivers in the NFL during the late 1950s and '60s. Sapp carried six straight times for 25 yards to the 1-yard line. After Britt was stopped for no gain, Sapp crashed off his right side into the end zone for a touchdown.

Sapp's score was Georgia's first touchdown against Georgia Tech since a 28–12 loss in 1953 and its first points of the season since a 14–13 setback to Alabama four weeks before. Ron Cooper's point after gave the Bulldogs a 7–0 lead with 2:17 remaining in the third quarter.

In the final quarter, the Yellow Jackets reached Georgia's 16-yard line, but a Bulldogs sack and an incomplete pass by Georgia Tech on fourth down turned the ball over to Georgia. Late in the game, Britt fumbled on his own 27-yard line, but Sapp recovered his teammate's mistake and likely saved the game. The Bulldogs held on for victory and snapped Georgia Tech's eight-year winning streak. As Coach Butts was carried to midfield to greet coach Bobby Dodd of Georgia Tech, writer Jesse Outlar observed, "In 19 years at Georgia, there had never been a happier moment for the little round man."

Besides Sapp's drought-breaking plunge into the end zone and his 91 rushing yards on 23 carries (Georgia's entire offense gained only 173 yards), he was also applauded for his dominating play on defense, including the fumble recovery which set up Georgia's scoring drive. Writer Furman Bisher reported the next day, Sapp had "chiseled his name in the granite alongside the name [sic] of great people who made themselves famous in this series...people like Frank Sinkwich and Charley Trippi."

In 1959, a year after his final season at Georgia, Sapp's jersey No. 40 joined Sinkwich's and Trippi's as the only football jerseys retired at the University of Georgia. Herschel Walker's jersey No. 34 followed 26 years later. Sapp's career at Georgia included being selected All-SEC as a junior and senior and gaining 1,265 career rushing yards (tied for 29th best at Georgia through 2006). However, the principal reason for his jersey joining Sinkwich's and Trippi's in retirement was because against hated Georgia Tech in 1957, Sapp became the drought-breaker.

The Best Losing Bulldogs Ever

On Thanksgiving Day 1957, two days prior to Georgia's celebrated win over Georgia Tech, Georgia's freshman team, the Bullpups, defeated Georgia Tech's Baby Jackets 13–7. With the victory, the Bullpups became the first freshman Georgia team to finish undefeated since the Fabulous Frosh of '39, which included Sinkwich, Lamar Davis, Walter Ruark, George Ellenson, Leo Costa, George Poschner, and many other memorable Bullpups later turned Bulldogs.

The 1957 Bullpups included standout linemen Pat Dye and Phil Ashe, halfbacks Fred Brown and Bobby Walden, and a talented, scrambling quarterback from Athens, Fran Tarkenton. Because of this young group, coupled with the varsity returnees who ended Georgia Tech's streak, the Bulldogs were considered one of the most improved teams for the 1958 season in the SEC, if not the entire nation.

The season did not begin as anticipated. Georgia lost its first three games, including just a five-point loss to number-11 Texas. It seemed that the inexperienced Georgia squad was trying so hard that it would force its own mistakes. "I don't know what to say," said Coach Butts following the 0–3 start. "Definitely the coaching job has been done, and the team seems to have a desire to win…but they just make so many mistakes."

Georgia entered its fourth game a slight underdog against Florida State in Jacksonville. The Seminoles were 3–1 and ran an "unorthodox" I formation on offense when most teams operated from the T formation. They fielded a quick backfield led by Bobby Renn, who was averaging 8.7 yards per carry.

In front of 16,023 spectators at the Gator Bowl, the Bulldogs unexpectedly led 14–0 at halftime on touchdown runs by Tommy Lewis and quarterback Charley Britt. For the first time in '58, Georgia was playing mistake-free football and did not commit a single turnover in the game. Florida State's Vic Prinzi and Renn passed for touchdowns in the second half, but the Bulldogs scored on runs by Brown and a second by Britt. Georgia won 28–13.

The Bulldogs scored on long drives of 61, 78, 63, and 81 yards to improve their all-time record to 4–0 versus the Seminoles. Georgia rushed for 278 yards and was led by Brown's 91 rushing yards on five carries, 59 yards on nine carries by Sapp, and Gene Littleton's 43 yards on 11 carries. Early in the game, Renn broke Florida State's all-time career rushing record held by his backfield coach, Lee Corso, currently a well-known college football analyst for ESPN.

Despite its critical win over Florida State, Georgia finished the season with a disappointing 4–6 record. However, the Bulldogs outscored their opponents 196–114, lost three games by one touchdown or less, and defeated Georgia Tech for a second straight season. Authors Ed Thilenius (Georgia football's play-by-play man at the time) and Jim Koger believed the 1958 Bulldogs "could be...the most powerful 'losing' team in the country" and foreshadowed the upcoming season: "For the juniors and their spunky sophomore playmates [of 1958], the unsuspecting Bulldogs of the '59 campaign, the best was yet to come. A good time would be had by all."

chapter 9

End of a Successful Era

Coach Butts chuckles as he explains his game plan to his 1959 squad in the week leading up to the Orange Bowl. Standing left to right are Jimmy Vickers, Fran Tarkenton, Pat Dye, and Don Soberdash. They finished 10–1 after beating Missouri in the bowl game.

Overachievers Topple Tide

Coach Wally Butts and his Bulldogs began the 1959 season with two relatively modest goals. First, they wanted to win their season-opening game, and second, they aspired to finish the year with more wins than losses. Georgia had not achieved either of these aspirations in the same season since 1954, and it did not appear likely it would do so in '59. The Bulldogs lost perhaps their two best players from the year before; center and linebacker Dave Lloyd departed for the NFL, while the drought-breaker, fullback Theron Sapp, graduated.

Quarterback Fran Tarkenton said years later, "There were many reasons the experts took us lightly." Most of the teams in the SEC kept their star players from 1958, Tarkenton added, "so [the experts] paid no attention to us. It is obvious why they rated us no higher than ninth [in the 12-team SEC] since we were 10th the previous year." During their preseason practices, however, the 1959 Bulldogs "were inspired by a cheering spirit and a determination that appeared lacking in previous years," as indicated by writer Charles Martin.

After two decades of facing Alabama in late October or early November, Georgia opened its season on September 19 against the Crimson Tide. Following four consecutive losing seasons, Alabama was 5–4–1 in '58 in Paul "Bear" Bryant's first season of coaching at his alma mater. Bryant began his second year with Alabama as one-point underdogs to Georgia before a near-capacity crowd in Sanford Stadium.

The Bulldogs scored first with 7:45 remaining in the opening quarter when sophomore Durward Pennington, on his first play as a member of Georgia's varsity, booted a 35-yard field goal. Georgia unexpectedly took a 10–0 lead following a 40-yard touchdown run by sophomore Bill "Taterbug" Godfrey on only his second carry as a varsity player. The touchdown was made possible by outstanding blocks by Pat Dye and Jimmy Vickers.

After receiving the second-half kickoff, Alabama drove 65 yards, consuming approximately 10 minutes of the clock, but was forced to settle for a field goal. Georgia clinched the victory by driving 74 yards in 10 plays in the final quarter for a touchdown. A one-yard sneak by Tarkenton and Pennington's point after gave the Bulldogs a 17–3 lead with 6:35 remaining in the game. There would be no more scoring. Georgia had accomplished the first of its two main goals.

Sophomores Pennington and Godfrey, along with quarterback Tarkenton and end Gorden Kelley, were instrumental in Georgia's season-beginning victory. Pennington was successful on a field goal and two point-after attempts and made a tackle on a kickoff. Godfrey rushed for 56 yards on only six carries, while Kelley caught five passes for 83 yards. Tarkenton, who did not start the game or any game in '59, for that matter, led a Bulldogs passing game that was almost perfect. He completed six of seven passes for 103 yards, while starter Charley Britt completed both of his two attempted passes for 21 yards. Georgia's defense held Alabama to only 217 total yards and was successful in keeping the Crimson Tide from crossing the goal line.

As Georgia players, coaches, boosters, and fans celebrated the victory after the game, Godfrey approached Coach Butts. Seemingly, according to Charles Martin, "During the wild hand-shaking on the field, an old grad or two must have put a bill or two in Godfrey's palm." Reportedly, Godfrey said to Butts, "Coach, ain't they good to you when you win?"

"We knew then we had a team that could win," Tarkenton said later.

Indeed, Georgia was a team that could win, defeating six of its next seven opponents to accomplish its second preseason goal. By mid-November, the Bulldogs were 7–1 and ranked 12th in the nation, with Auburn and Georgia Tech still remaining on the regular-season schedule.

The Day Sanford Shook

After Georgia's 21–10 defeat of Florida on November 7, 1959, a telephone call was immediately made by Georgia football business manager Howell Hollis to the Sanford Stadium's groundskeeper.

Hollis indicated that every available seat needed to be inserted in the stadium for the Bulldogs' game the following week against eighth-ranked Auburn, one of the most anticipated contests in Georgia football history.

For only the second time beginning in 1916, the Georgia-Auburn game was not played in neutral Columbus, Georgia—the 26,000 seats of Memorial Stadium could no longer accommodate the larger crowds the game was attracting. Henceforth, the yearly rivalry game was to be played on a home-and-home basis. For the game against Auburn in '59, 55,000 to 60,000 spectators somehow jammed into Sanford Stadium. Every single seat was taken, with many fans standing wherever they could find space.

In the first quarter, Ed Dyas's 43-yard field goal gave Auburn a 3–0 advantage. Georgia's Britt fumbled a punt in the following quarter, which led to a second Dyas field goal and a 6–0 lead for Auburn at halftime. Britt received another punt in the second half and, this time without error, streaked 39 yards for Georgia's first points. Pennington's point after gave the Bulldogs a one-point lead.

While Georgia was punting deep from its own territory in the final quarter, Britt backed into teammate Bobby Walden's punt. Auburn's Joe Leichtnam recovered the ball, and quarterback Bryant Harvard soon followed with a sneak for a touchdown. The Tigers held a 13–7 lead with only 6:30 remaining in the game.

Auburn had possession of the ball late in the contest and was trying to run out the clock. On a rollout on third down, Harvard was struck by Bill Herron and fumbled. Pat Dye recovered the ball for Georgia at Auburn's 35-yard line, and the Bulldogs had new life.

Following two consecutive errant passing attempts by Tarkenton, the junior quarterback completed two successive passes to Don Soberdash for a combined 25 yards. After two more plays, Tarkenton and the offense faced fourth down and goal on Auburn's 13-yard line with 30 seconds remaining. What followed next, as written by Charles Martin, thrilled "thousands of Georgians who found themselves slapping backs and kissing people they didn't know, not only all over the stands but before radios and TVs throughout the land."

Tarkenton rolled to his right, stopped, and lofted a pass across the field to a waiting Herron, who caught the ball on the 2-yard line and crossed the goal line. The game was tied 13–13 with only 20 seconds left in the contest. Years later, Tarkenton recalled the play and confessed, "At that moment, I didn't even know it was fourth down."

The Kick Is Up, and It Is Good!

Following Tarkenton's game-tying touchdown pass to Herron against Auburn in 1959, Pennington came on to the field to attempt the extra point and, hopefully for Georgia, break the 13–13 tie. A collected Pennington calmly nailed the point after, and the Bulldogs had a one-point lead with seconds remaining in the game. After the contest, a reporter asked Pennington if he had been nervous prior to the kick. Pennington answered, "Frankly, no. I thought we were ahead 13–12. I didn't realize until after I had kicked the point that the score was tied."

Following the ensuing kickoff, Auburn's Richard Wood threw a long desperation pass that fell incomplete. After winning three SEC titles, from 1942 to 1948, the Georgia Bulldogs had captured their first conference crown in 11 years. Writer Furman Bisher described the postgame celebration: "Strangers hugged and kissed strangers. Small children raced out on the field to grasp their heroes, wearing the red shirts which their own sweat had turned the rich color of blood."

In an elated Georgia locker room following the Bulldog victory, end Vickers explained, "It was a case of everybody sticking together and not giving up. We just wouldn't be beaten." Guard Dye asserted, "Let me tell you something. That Auburn is the best team I ever played against." Ironically, Dye would become a very successful head coach at Auburn 22 years later, from 1981 to 1992.

Dye continued, "They have got 11 All-Americans out there, and they are the number-one team in the country."

"Behind us," Vickers corrected.

"Right," said Dye. "Behind us."

It was said that the two worst traffic jams in Athens in more than a decade occurred on the very same day. Traffic stretched bumper to bumper for more than eight miles from Sanford Stadium before and after Georgia's momentous win over Auburn. This should sound familiar to present day Bulldog followers.

Georgia ended its 1959 season by defeating Georgia Tech then Missouri in the Orange Bowl. The Bulldogs finished 10–1 and ranked fifth in the nation. This was a far cry from a team hoping to just finish with more wins than losses and picked by pre-season prognosticators no better than ninth in their conference.

"I shall always have a warm feeling for this football team," Coach Butts said years afterward. "I would say they exploited maximum ability more than any of my teams."

Dye's Blocks Send Butts Out a Winner

Prior to the 1960 season, the Associated Press poll had Georgia ranked for the first time since the preseason rankings began being released in 1950. Most of the Bulldogs' standout players from the 1959 championship squad returned, including three of the four players—Tarkenton, Dye, and Walden—selected first- or second-team All-SEC in '59. What followed the high expectations for 1960 were mostly disappointments, as Georgia had only a 5–4 record heading into its 55th meeting against rival Georgia Tech. The Yellow Jackets had an identical record but were only 10 points from being unbeaten, having lost three of their four games by only one or two points.

The University of Georgia dedicated the game to Harry Mehre, an *Atlanta Journal* columnist and former Georgia head coach (1928–1937) who never lost to Georgia Tech at Sanford Stadium. Eleven Georgia seniors would be playing their final collegiate game, including quarterback and captain Tarkenton, considered perhaps the most dangerous college passer in the nation. There was no possibility for an SEC title for either team or any kind of bowl game, just bragging rights for the state of Georgia in front of 55,000 in attendance. The Bulldogs were favored by one and a half points prior to kickoff. As it turned out, the so-called "experts" were nearly correct.

With 4:09 remaining until halftime in a scoreless game, Georgia Tech's Marvin Tibbetts scored from the 1-yard line, capping a drive that began late in the opening quarter. Dye blocked Tommy Wells's conversion attempt, whereby the kicked ball literally hit Dye in the face. Just before halftime, Wells missed a 38-yard field goal that was partially blocked by Dye, and the Bulldogs were fortunate to be losing by only 6–0 at the half.

Late in the third quarter, a pass by Georgia Tech's Stan Gann was picked off by Bill McKenney and returned 23 yards to the Yellow Jackets' 13-yard line. Five plays later and with 14:26 remaining in the game, Bill Godfrey dove into the end zone for a Georgia score. Pennington's successfully kicked extra point was his 16th consecutive—three shy of the SEC record established eight years before by Georgia Tech's Pepper Rodgers.

With eight minutes left in the game, the Yellow Jackets moved from their 32-yard line to Georgia's 13 in eight plays. The offense stalled, and Wells was called upon to attempt a 30-yard field goal with approximately four minutes remaining. Wells's kick was wide far to the left. The Bulldogs would eventually be forced to punt, but on Tech's last drive of the game, Tarkenton intercepted a Yellow Jackets pass to secure a 7–6 Bulldogs victory. It was the first time Georgia had defeated Georgia Tech in four consecutive seasons since 1913 and the days of the Red and Black's first All-American, Bob McWhorter.

Besides intercepting his team-leading third interception of the 1960 season, Tarkenton struggled, as did the entire Georgia offense. He completed nine of 14 passes for only 65 yards, was intercepted twice, and rushed for two yards on eight carries. Notwithstanding, Tarkenton ended his collegiate career as a winner before pursuing a stellar professional career for 18 seasons in the NFL.

In what would turn out to be his final coached game, Georgia's Butts was proud of his winning team: "[The] Georgia players showed tremendous desire to win all the way, and I think the victory made it a successful season for us."

Coach Calls It Quits

On December 23, 1960, Butts resigned as the University of Georgia's head football coach after a successful 22-season stint. It was noted that the "Little Round Man," "Little Spartan," or "Mr. Five-by-Five," if you prefer, would rank with golfer Bobby Jones and baseball's Ty Cobb among Georgia's sports immortals. Butts, who would remain at the university as the school's athletic

Coach Butts is carried off the field after the Bulldogs' 14–0 victory over Missouri in the Orange Bowl on January 1, 1960.

director, wanted to devote more time to his immediate family and grandchildren.

Butts announced his retirement while preparing to coach the South All-Stars in the annual Blue-Gray Game on December 31. "There's nothing I can do now that I haven't done before," said Butts. "I've been a head coach for 32 years [including 10 years in high school]....That's long enough to be in the coaching business."

Georgia's list of possible successors for Butts was long. Former Bulldog greats and college assistant coaches Charley Trippi and John Rauch were possibilities. Florida's defensive coordinator Jack Green and Oliver Hunnicutt, a Georgia letterman in the late 1930s and coach at LaGrange High School, were also contenders. However, the two leading prospects were another Florida assistant, Gene Ellenson, and Georgia assistant Johnny Griffith, both members of Bulldog SEC championship teams from the 1940s.

Here's Johnny...

As soon as Wally Butts resigned from Georgia's head coaching position, the University of Georgia's president, Dr. O.C. Aderhold, immediately began searching for a replacement. According to author Jesse Outlar, "Dr. Aderhold held a secret meeting with Ellenson at the Waycross home of George Fesperman, a member of the athletic board. Dr. Aderhold decided that Ellenson was his coach." Ellenson was a member of Georgia's "Fabulous Frosh of '39," the starting left tackle on the 1942 national championship squad, a Florida assistant coach, and was well known for his motivational speeches.

Ellenson was interviewed by a Jacksonville, Florida, newspaper, and he mentioned several changes he would like to make if he became Georgia's head coach. His remarks were, according to Outlar, "misinterpreted." In a single newspaper interview, "Ellenson had talked himself out of one of the most sought-after jobs in football."

Johnny Griffith was Aderhold's second choice and was offered the head job. Griffith played halfback for the Bulldogs in 1946 and, prior to becoming Georgia's 21st head coach, was the Bulldogs' freshman coach and coordinator of the recruiting program. At the time of his hire, the 36-year old Griffith was the SEC's second-youngest head football coach.

Georgia began its 1961 season on September 23 hosting Alabama, and Griffith was nowhere to be found on the Bulldogs' sidelines. He was confined to a bed at Athens General Hospital undergoing an emergency appendectomy. This might have been an omen of the misfortune to follow for Coach Griffith and his teams. With assistant John Gregory serving as acting head coach, Georgia, only a seven-point underdog to Alabama, was annihilated 32–6.

The Bulldogs' offense was held to five first downs and 112 total offensive yards. The lone bright spot for Georgia was the performance of newcomer Larry Rakestraw, the Bulldogs' backup quarterback to Jake Saye. The sophomore Rakestraw completed four of four passes for 44 yards and led the squad in rushing with 13 yards on five carries. From the hospital, Coach Griffith had planned to follow the game by radio but apparently slept through the 26-point loss.

Back on the sideline for the following week's game against Vanderbilt, Griffith and his Dogs were upset and shut out 21–0. The Bulldogs had been a touchdown favorite but could not stop Commodore quarterback Hank Lesesne. An Atlanta native, Lesesne completed nine of 11 passes for 81 yards and three touchdowns while rushing for 41 yards.

Beginning with a victory over South Carolina on October 7, the '61 Bulldogs won three of their next four games but would drop the final four contests to finish with a discouraging 3–7 record.

One Shining Moment

By mid-November of 1962, Georgia had won just two of nine games for the season, including ties against South Carolina, Kentucky, and North Carolina State. Auburn, a certain loss, was next on the schedule for Coach Griffith's struggling Bulldogs. The Tigers were 6–1, seeking a conference championship, and a 10-point favorite to defeat Georgia at home. On the arms of quarterbacks Mailon Kent and Jimmy Sidle, Auburn led the conference in passing and was looking to even its series with the Bulldogs, who held a 30–29–6 Georgia advantage. On the Tigers' coaching staff were assistants Joel Eaves, Vince Dooley, and Erk Russell—names of individuals who would soon become very familiar to Georgia football.

In 1962, the Bulldogs' running game was nearly nonexistent, perhaps the worst in Georgia history. The offense was carried by quarterback Larry Rakestraw. He had recently become only the seventh player in school history to surpass 1,000 total yards in a season. While Auburn was hoping to further position itself for only its second SEC title ever, Georgia had little to gain and absolutely nothing to lose.

After a scoreless opening quarter before 35,000 fans at Cliff Hare Stadium on a wet day, Auburn's Billy Edge intercepted a Jake Saye pass and returned it 46 yards for a score. Saye was soon benched, and Georgia tied the score following a Rakestraw touchdown pass to halfback Don Porterfield. The Tigers, however, led 14–7 at halftime after a three-yard scoring run by fullback Larry Laster.

At halftime, sophomore Joe Burson had asked assistant coach Bobby Proctor if he could gamble and try for an interception since Auburn kept throwing to Burson's short man during the first half. Proctor agreed but warned, "Don't you dare try it unless you're sure you can intercept. If you miss that ball, it'll be an Auburn touchdown."

In the second half, Rakestraw found Porterfield again, and Georgia tied the score. Bulldogs kicker Bill McCullough gave Georgia the lead in the fourth quarter when he kicked a 48-yard field goal—at the time, the second-longest field goal in team history. Georgia seemingly clinched a victory when Burson succeeded at intercepting a Kent pass and raced 87 yards for a score. With 8:21 remaining, the Bulldogs led 24–14.

After Burson's score, the game was far from over. The Tigers pulled within three points with 4:53 left in the contest and later got the ball back. However, a Tucker Frederickson fumble was recovered by Georgia on Auburn's 9-yard line, and, three plays later, Rakestraw threw his third touchdown to Porterfield.

The Bulldogs defeated the Tigers for only the second time in 10 years in a 30–21 victory. Rakestraw led all rushers and passers with 167 yards passing on 12 of 21 attempts and 54 rushing yards on 19 carries. Auburn head coach Ralph Jordan said that the Georgia quarterback was the best his team had faced all season and added, "This much I do know. Georgia just gave us a good, old-fashioned licking, a physical beating. I salute them for their good play."

Although Auburn's offense had 23 first downs and outgained Georgia in total yardage (334–281), the Tigers committed four turnovers that ultimately led to their downfall. Coach Griffith commented after the win, "It was our best game of the season." It would actually be Georgia's best game of the three seasons comprising Griffith's head coaching career.

chapter 10

Dooley Restores Winning Tradition

Vince Dooley gives his team a pep talk before practice after their arrival in Dallas for the 1966 Cotton Bowl game against Southern Methodist University. Dooley became the most successful football coach in Georgia history, winning a national title and six Southeastern Conference championships.

Vince Who?

When Johnny Griffith resigned as Georgia's head coach on December 4, 1963, he departed with a disappointing 10–16–4 overall record for the seasons 1961 through 1963. All three of Griffith's seasons were losing campaigns, continuing a trend whereby the Bulldogs experienced seven losing seasons over a nine-year span (1955–1963). Griffith's lack of success included a 1–8 record against rivals Florida, Auburn, and Georgia Tech.

Georgia's athletic director, newly hired Joel Eaves, had previously built a winning basketball program at Auburn for 14 seasons and had also served as an assistant for the school's football team. At Auburn, Eaves had instructed and coached alongside Vince Dooley—the quarterback and captain of the Tigers' 1953 football squad and head freshman team coach from 1961 to 1963. Eaves had felt for some time that the 31-year-old Dooley would make an outstanding coach and asked him to come to Athens to accept the Georgia head coaching position. Dooley said years later, "Joel did not want anyone to know I was in Athens, and that posed no problem. At that time it was very easy for me not to be recognized. Nobody knew me."

Vince Dooley was hired as the new Bulldogs coach on the same day of Griffith's resignation. He also had been working on a Ph.D. in history at Auburn before signing a four-year contract at Georgia. Based on the approving endorsement Eaves gave the young coach, writer Loran Smith speculated, "His future as a head coach seems so promising that he may never get a doctorate."

On the day he was hired, Dooley, who would begin his head coaching career as the second-youngest coach in the SEC, said, "I dreamed of being a head coach, but my ambitions have come a lot faster than I expected."

A Failed First Outing

As the 1964 season opener against Alabama loomed, Georgia alumni were anxious for a winning campaign after 15 seasons

(1949–1963) of more losses than wins. The Crimson Tide may have been the best team in college football over the previous few years and were coming off a 1963 Sugar Bowl championship season. Although the Bulldogs were 21-point underdogs to Alabama at Tuscaloosa, Coach Dooley felt Georgia actually had a slight chance for victory because his team was well conditioned and the Bulldogs showed signs of being good defensively.

In front of 43,000 spectators on a Saturday night at Denny Stadium, Georgia began its '64 season and Vince Dooley his head coaching career against coach Paul "Bear" Bryant, quarterback Joe Namath, and the rest of the mighty Alabama squad in the 50th meeting between the schools. Interestingly, Bulldog captains for the contest were not from Georgia: halfback Wayne Swinford and fullback Leon Armbrester were from Alabama, and tackle Ray Rissmiller was from Pennsylvania.

In the second quarter, a 26-yard field goal by Georgia's Bob Etter reduced Alabama's lead to 7–3, however the Crimson Tide then exploded for 24 unanswered points and a 31–3 victory. The Bulldogs' once encouraging defense yielded 407 yards, while the offense struggled to gain 170. Namath was brilliant, completing 16 of 21 passes for 167 yards and rushing for 55 yards and three scores.

About the only humorous episode in an otherwise discouraging weekend took place the night before the game. Dressed in blue blazers, the team was feasting on 16-ounce steaks at the Stafford Hotel. Dooley, athletic director Eaves, and assistant coach Erk Russell talked while drinking coffee nearby. Another friend involved in the conversation commented, "I came in from the airport with a one-armed taxi driver. He said he was taking the points and Georgia [over Alabama]." Russell responded, "That's how he lost his arm."

The next week, Georgia played at Vanderbilt and was predicted to lose to the only SEC team it was favored to defeat in the preseason. Bulldogs quarterback Lynn Hughes scored on a one-yard run following a key interception by end Barry Wilson and Georgia won a defensive standoff 7–0. Dooley's defense played beyond its potential in holding the Commodores to no points and 199 yards.

Georgia's defense, which seemed rather promising in the pre-season, carried the Bulldogs throughout the year as it played a major role in helping to achieve a 7–3–1 record. The Georgia defenders allowed only three teams to score more than eight points and recorded three shutouts, including in the final two games against Georgia Tech then Texas Tech in the Sun Bowl.

Dooley was named the SEC's Coach of the Year by the United Press International News. The young coach may have begun his Georgia head coaching career similarly to Griffith by being devastated by Alabama. It soon became apparent, however, that Dooley's career as a head coach was destined for far greater success.

Turning Tears into Triumph

Georgia's record stood at 1–1–1 after a 7–7 tie with a lackluster South Carolina team on October 3, 1964. The deadlock with the Gamecocks reduced senior Wayne Swinford to tears. When defensive backfield coach Hootie Ingram asked Swinford what was the matter, he responded, "Coach, I've never been on a winning team at Georgia, and we've got a chance to do it and can't even beat South Carolina."

The following week, the Bulldogs upset favored Clemson in Athens 19–7. Swinford, who entered the game leading the nation in kickoff returns, returned a Tiger punt 59 yards, setting up a Bob Etter field goal. He also intercepted a pass. After the game, Clemson coach Frank Howard commented on Swinford's blazing speed: "If we could have caught that damn rabbit we could have won."

Swinford was one of two Bulldogs named to the AP's first team All-SEC in 1964. He finished tied for first on the team with three interceptions and was third in the nation in punt returns, with 343 yards on 34 returns. More importantly, Swinford was an integral part of coach Dooley's first Georgia team, which had the second-best record at the school in 16 seasons, going back to 1949.

'Bama Fooled by Flea-Flicker

A couple days prior to Georgia's first game of the 1965 season, Coach Dooley addressed the Athens Touchdown Club. While presenting his coaching staff, Dooley announced, "As I introduce them [the coaches], I want them to get up and go back to the office and continue to get ready for Alabama." As was the case the previous season, Georgia would likely have its hands full again with the Crimson Tide…and perhaps the entire schedule.

Although the 1965 Bulldogs were expected to be better than the seven-win squad from the year before, they were predicted by most to win only four or five games and finish in the bottom third of the conference. Besides Alabama, Georgia's

Vince Dooley is carried on the shoulders of his team members after a memorable victory early in his career at Georgia, which catapulted the Bulldogs back into the national spotlight. Players are Ken Whiddon (65), Gary Adams (86), Kent Lawrence (24), and fullback Brad Johnson (41).

challenging schedule also included Michigan and Florida State—each team suffered only one loss in '64. Alabama had finished the previous regular season undefeated, ranked first in the nation, had outscored the Bulldogs 151–22 in the last five meetings (1960–1964) between the two schools, and was a two-touchdown favorite to defeat Georgia in Athens.

On a hot and humid afternoon, 41,500 spectators occupied Sanford Stadium while ABC broadcast the game throughout the Southeast. Georgia's Bob Etter kicked a 37-yard field goal in the second quarter for the contest's first score. On the ensuing drive, Crimson Tide quarterback Steve Sloan was hit by Jerry Varnado and Jiggy Smaha and was separated from the ball. The ball wobbled into the hands of tackle George Patton, who ran 55 yards for a Georgia touchdown. The Bulldogs led 10–0 early in the second quarter.

By the end of the third quarter, Alabama had tied the game 10–10 following a David Ray field goal and an eight-yard run by Steve Bowman. Later, Sloan capped an 11-play, 74-yard drive with 3:14 remaining in the game by scoring on a two-yard rollout. The Crimson Tide had scored 17 consecutive points and appeared to be on their way to victory.

What transpired on the ensuing drive is one of the most memorable plays in Georgia football history. With a portion of the Sanford Stadium crowd heading for the exits early to avoid postgame traffic, Georgia quarterback Kirby Moore fired a short hook pass from his 27-yard line to end Pat Hodgson. Hodgson caught the ball just beyond Georgia's 35-yard line and lateraled it to halfback Bob Taylor, who was trailing the play. Taylor, with ball in hand, streaked down the left sideline for a 73-yard flea-flicker touchdown. The Bulldogs had cut Alabama's lead to 17–16 with 2:08 left in the contest. "We worked on the play, and Coach Dooley called for it [the flea-flicker]," Taylor said after the game. "Everything just went perfect."

Dooley decided to not kick the extra-point and instead attempted a two-point conversion to go for the win. Sophomore Moore rolled out to his right and completed the conversion pass to a wide-open Hodgson. Georgia had retaken the lead 18–17.

Alabama had one more opportunity on offense. Following a deep kickoff return by the Crimson Tide, they moved to Georgia's 26-yard line on three Sloan completions and two converted fourth-down runs by Bowman. With 14 seconds remaining in the game, Ray missed a 42-yard field goal that was wide and short, and the Bulldogs were victorious by a single point.

Moore, Georgia's backup quarterback from Dothan, Alabama, finished the game with 43 rushing yards on 10 carries and 99 passing yards on three of four passes, including the miraculous 73-yard flea-flicker. Nearly one-third of Georgia's total offense (229 yards) was gained on the extraordinary play. Coach Dooley discussed the play after game: "I want you to know that I got it from Georgia Tech four years ago. I thank them very much right now."

For more than four decades an ongoing controversy has existed as to whether Hodgson's knee was grounded after he caught Moore's pass and before he lateraled the ball to Taylor. If this did occur, and it appears likely as revealed later in game photos, the 73-yard play instead should have gone for about 10 yards. Nevertheless, the phenomenal flea-flicker counted, and Georgia handed Alabama what would eventually be its only loss of the season.

David Slays Goliath

Following victories over Alabama and Vanderbilt to start the 1965 season, Georgia was ranked 10th in the nation—its first appearance in the Associated Press poll since the 1960 preseason. The Bulldogs next traveled to Ann Arbor, Michigan, to face seventh-ranked Michigan, the defending Big Ten and Rose Bowl champions. Following Georgia's unlikely success in 1964 and the inconceivable victory over Alabama to open the season, many concluded that the undersized and inexperienced Bulldogs would soon run out of miracles. Georgia had played once before at Michigan in 1957 and was blanked 26–0. A similar result was expected eight years later.

The Bulldogs had never faced a team the size of the Wolverines. Georgia was outweighed by an average of more than 15 pounds per man. Linemen Steve Smith, Charles Kines, and Tom Mack all weighed between 230 and 240 pounds—very large sizes more than years ago in college football. Georgia's largest player, sophomore Smaha, weighed only 225 pounds, and he had just recently became a starter after an injury to Jimmy Cooley.

The Wolverines were looking to extend an eight-game winning streak in front of a raucous crowd at Michigan Stadium, now commonly referred to as the "Big House." The stadium's capacity was an enormous 103,219—with an average attendance of nearly 80,000 in 1965—but only 59,470 spectators showed up for the game against Georgia. There was speculation that many Wolverine fans stayed home because Michigan was thought to be playing an inferior Georgia team, and they wanted to rest up for Michigan's visitor the following week, rival Michigan State.

Late in the opening quarter, Georgia's Etter kicked a 34-yard field goal into a northern wind. However, Michigan quickly took a 7–3 advantage following a one-yard scoring run by Tim Radigan. With one second remaining in the first half, Etter made a 44-yard field goal, and the Bulldogs trailed by only one point at halftime.

In the fourth quarter, the Bulldogs generated a 51-yard scoring drive highlighted by a spectacular 23-yard run by quarterback Preston Ridlehuber. From Michigan's 29-yard line, Ridlehuber rolled to his left, faked a pass, completely changed direction rolling to his right, and followed four blockers to the Wolverines' 6-yard line. One play and a Georgia penalty later, Ridlehuber passed 10 yards to Pat Hodgson for a Bulldogs touchdown.

Losing 12–7, Michigan began to move toward Georgia's goal until a Dick Vidmer pass was intercepted by Lynn Hughes and returned 38 yards. With only 1:50 remaining in the game, the 150-pound Etter, or "the biggest little man in the stadium today," according to Dooley, added a 31-yard field goal for Georgia, en route to a 15–7 victory.

The "Cinderella Dogs," or "Dooley's Demons," as some referred to them, had pulled yet another upset win. The Dogs were guided by their alternating quarterbacks, Ridlehuber (61 rushing yards, 28 passing) and Moore (four of six passes, 52 yards, 43-yard punt average), while Bob Taylor led all rushers with 71 yards on 13 carries. Georgia's defense was simply too quick for Michigan's massive offensive line and limited the Wolverines to 235 total yards.

Not only did the win by the Bulldogs garner prestige for the Georgia football program, but it brought pride to the SEC and all of southern football. "I just can't say whether this was a greater victory than our 18–17 victory over Alabama in the opener," said a beaming Dooley. "This is a great one for us. It means even more because we pulled it off in their backyard."

On the following week, Georgia defeated Clemson by two touchdowns in Athens. In the October 11 Associated Press rankings, the Bulldogs were fifth in the nation (two voters had actually ranked them number one). Dooley's Demons had won nine of their last 10 games dating back to 1964, the school's best stretch since the '59 conference championship squad. The University of Georgia football team was unpredictably and surprisingly among college football's elite.

How Do You Spell Relief?

Georgia rebounded from a satisfactory 6–4 season in 1965 to have its best campaign the following year since the 1940s. The 1966 Bulldogs were 10–1 overall, SEC champions for the first of six times under the Dooley regime, defeated SMU 24–9 in the Cotton Bowl, and finished with a number-four Associated Press ranking—their best in 20 years.

Much of Georgia's success in 1966 can be attributed to its quick and harassing defense. The Bulldog defenders allowed fewer than nine points per game for the season, held to 2.3 yards per rushing attempt, intercepted 25 passes, and featured stand-out lineman Patton and Bill Stanfill and safety-man Lynn Hughes.

For the senior Hughes, safety was not the only position on the field where he succeeded at Georgia.

On Dooley's first Georgia team, Hughes played quarterback and led the Bulldogs with 408 passing yards. Prior to his junior season, Hughes was moved to defense because Georgia had considerable depth at quarterback with experienced Ridlehuber and the emergence of sophomore Moore. Hughes responded at his new position by intercepting a conference-leading six passes and being selected first team AP and UPI All-SEC defensive back.

Prior to the 1965 Kentucky game, Ridlehuber had been switched to halfback because of Georgia's lack of depth at the position. During the contest, Moore was lost because of a severe broken nose. After the injury, Hughes moved over from defense and was inserted as Georgia's quarterback. Although the Bulldogs eventually lost to the Wildcats, Hughes was impressive at his old position, completing four of five passes for 58 yards.

Almost exactly a year later, in 1966, Hughes would get another chance to quarterback Georgia against Kentucky. The Bulldogs were losing 15–14 late in the third quarter when starter Moore injured his ankle and had to leave the game. Coach Dooley decided against putting in second-string Rick Arrington, who had played substantially in each of Georgia's first five games of the year. Hughes, who had not played quarterback since the Kentucky game of 1965, spelled relief for Moore because of his "experience," according to Dooley.

Hughes promptly drove Georgia 53 yards in seven plays while rushing for a 10-yard touchdown. Having recaptured the lead, Georgia decided to attempt a two-point conversion. End Kent Lawrence ran from the sideline into the huddle with the called play written on a sheet of paper. Hughes passed to Sandy Johnson for the two points, and the Bulldogs led 22–15. Later in the quarter, Hughes drove the offense down the field again for an Etter field goal.

In the 27–15 defeat of Kentucky, Hughes rushed and passed for 59 yards in seven plays, but most importantly, led a Georgia comeback from a position he had not played for an entire year.

"Lynn Hughes never ceases to amaze me," said Coach Dooley following the Bulldogs' victory. "He has not practiced or played one offensive play this season, but when he is called on for the big effort…well, you saw what he did."

One week later, Hughes, the all-conference safety, did not play on defense but instead made his first start at quarterback in two seasons. Against North Carolina, he completed five of 10 passes for 95 yards in a 28–3 Georgia win.

Moore recuperated in time for the Bulldogs' next game against Florida and returned to quarterback Georgia for the rest of the year. Hughes would see some action under center again late in the season against Auburn but primarily finished out 1966 playing his familiar safety position. For the season, he intercepted four passes and was named first-team All-SEC for the second consecutive year at defensive back. However, Hughes may be best remembered for what he did as Georgia's quarterback in relief.

"You'd never know he'd been on the defensive unit," Dooley said of Hughes, "for he grabbed the controls in spectacular fashion."

Success in '68

By the 1968 season, Coach Dooley had brought a once struggling Georgia football program back to the prominence it enjoyed prior to the 1950s. The Bulldogs had also grown in popularity, as nearly 20,000 seats were added to Sanford Stadium in 1967 to enlarge its capacity to 59,000.

Admission to home games against prominent opponents became prime tickets. At Vittorio's restaurant in Atlanta, author Jesse Outlar recalled, Loran Smith of the university was entertaining some members of the media and Bulldogs fans, John Smith and Corn White.

"Corn, I would like for you to meet Loran Smith," introduced John Smith. White casually responded, "Hello, Mr. Smith." John Smith barked, "Corn, Mr. Smith is the Georgia ticket man. He handles all those Georgia tickets." White then excitedly exclaimed,

"My God, John, why didn't you say so? How are you, Mr. Smith? Vittorio, order everybody a round of drinks on me."

As was the case with Dooley's first four teams, Georgia in 1968 had an unyielding defense, excellent special teams play, and a reliable running game. In addition, for the first time during Coach Dooley's tenure, the Bulldogs displayed a potent passing attack. Newcomer Mike Cavan and junior Donnie Hampton combined to pass for the second-most yards in school history (1,929), with no Georgia team throwing more until 1991. A band of gifted receivers, most notably newcomer Charlie Whittemore, were known for their great hands and clutch catches.

Although only sophomores, Cavan and Whittemore immediately began threatening school passing and receiving records. Against Clemson, Georgia's 300 passing yards were the third most in school history. Three weeks later versus Vanderbilt, the Bulldogs passed for 261 more yards, while Whittemore was on

Vince Dooley discusses strategy with his team as workers pull a tarp over the field the week prior to the 1969 Sugar Bowl game against Arkansas in New Orleans.

the receiving end of eight passes for 146 yards—eighth most in school history.

Led by tackle Bill Stanfill, safety Jake Scott, end Billy Payne, and linebacker Happy Dicks, the Bulldogs' defense was third best in the nation in total defense and ranked first in scoring defense. Against Vanderbilt, Georgia held the Commodores' rushing attack to 28 yards on 28 carries. Vanderbilt's quarterback, John Miller, completed half of his 26 passes against the Bulldogs for 154 yards and was intercepted three times. Nevertheless, Dooley commented after the 32–6 Georgia victory that Miller was the "finest scrambling quarterback I've ever seen."

"Tell Coach Dooley I appreciate that, I really do," said Miller. "But you can also tell Coach I'd appreciate him keeping ol' Bill Stanfill and Happy Dicks offa me some, too."

Dooley has said that he never coached a better athlete than Jake Scott. Against Kentucky in 1968, Scott returned two intercepted passes for touchdowns. Only one other player in the history of the SEC has accomplished this feat, while only one player in NCAA history has ever returned three interceptions for scores in a single game.

The Bulldogs finished the 1968 regular season with an 8–0–2 record. This was only the third of six times in school history to date that Georgia had accomplished an undefeated regular season. The Dogs were expected to easily handle co–Southwest Conference champion Arkansas in the Sugar Bowl on January 1, 1969. However, Georgia committed eight turnovers on a chilly day in New Orleans and lost to the Razorbacks 16–2.

Following the Bulldogs' first defeat of 1968, according to Outlar, a New Orleans taxi driver cheered up a group of saddened Georgia followers. He said with a straight face, "I don't understand what happened to that Georgia team. When I brought several of them to the hotel at 2:00 AM this morning, they told me there was no way they could lose to Arkansas."

chapter 11

Times of Adjustment and a State of Rebuilding

Vince Dooley instructs his All-American lineman Royce Smith during practice before the 1971 Gator Bowl against North Carolina and Tar Heels coach Bill Dooley.

Integration of Five Pioneers

Monday, October 4, 1971, is a memorable and special date in the history of University of Georgia football. On that particular afternoon, Georgia's freshman team, the Bullpups, defeated Clemson's junior varsity in Death Valley 33–3. This game was of significance because of the makeup of the Bullpup team. In victory, Georgia was led by outstanding performances from tailback Horace King, linebacker Clarence Pope, and cornerback Larry West, three of the first five African American football recruits at Georgia, who were playing in their first collegiate game.

African Americans began playing college football soon after the inception of the sport in the early 1900s. However, integrated teams were limited to the northeast portion of the United States, later including the Midwest. By the middle of the century, black players attended a number of schools throughout the entire country, except in the South. During this time, not only were African Americans not allowed to play at traditionally white, southern schools, but blacks at northern colleges and universities usually could not participate when playing on the road in the South.

In 1956, Prentice Gautt of Oklahoma became the first African American scholarship football player at a school in the South. Nevertheless, by 1965, of the 24,000 black students enrolled at formerly all-white southern colleges, none played on any of the schools' football teams. By 1970, however, southern campuses expanded African American enrollment to nearly 100,000 students. As the black population at southern colleges grew, so did the pressure applied by student groups to recruit African American football players.

In 1968, wingback Lester McClain of Tennessee became the first black player in the SEC to participate in a varsity collegiate football game. The University of Georgia soon followed suit and signed King, Pope, West, Chuck Kinnebrew, and Richard Appleby to its freshman class of 1971. Of the five African American recruits, King, Pope, and Appleby were signees from Athens, with King being the first African American to sign with Georgia.

King recognized that freshman coach John Donaldson and Vince Dooley made sure everything ran smoothly as he joined the team. "Coach Donaldson told me from the start that he had confidence in me and that I could play," King later said. "His encouragement meant a lot, and he made me feel he understood my problems."

Georgia football's first African Americans had significant impact in the Bullpups' 30-point blowout victory over Clemson. King rushed for 143 yards on 25 carries and a touchdown and also threw for a 38-yard score. West intercepted three Tigers passes and returned one for a touchdown. From his linebacker position, Pope called the defensive signals. For the five-game freshman season of '71, King rushed for a remarkable 829 yards and nine touchdowns. He also led the team in punt returns, kickoff returns, and was second in receiving. West led the team with four interceptions.

Although Richard Appleby was declared ineligible in 1971, he would lead Georgia in receiving in all three of his varsity seasons (1973–1975) and was selected all-conference as a junior in 1974. Pope, Kinnebrew, and West were each one-year starters as Bulldogs. During his career as a Bulldog, West intercepted six passes, including one he returned 75 yards for a touchdown against Vanderbilt in 1972.

While at Georgia, King would become a household name. He was a three-year starter for the Bulldogs at wingback and tailback and rushed for 1,287 career yards and 19 touchdowns. He was a sixth-round selection of the NFL's Detroit Lions, where he would play for nine seasons, from 1975 to 1983.

On August 31, 2002, at Sanford Stadium, Georgia's first African American football players were honored during pregame ceremonies at the Georgia-Clemson game. It was difficult to imagine that only 32 years before, no African American had yet to don the Red and Black in the very same stadium. In their time at Georgia, King, Kinnebrew, West, Pope, and Appleby became brave pioneers in breaking the racial barriers that had traditionally excluded blacks from participation on previous Georgia football teams.

The Drive

Following 1968, which was regarded as one of the more success-ful seasons in Georgia football history, the Bulldogs sank into mediocrity. Georgia posted 5–5–1 and 5–5 records in 1969 and 1970, including two losses to Georgia Tech.

To begin the 1971 season, Georgia abruptly recorded nine consecutive victories and was ranked seventh in the country by mid-November. The Bulldogs' senior-laden defense shut out four of their first nine opponents and held all but one to one touchdown or less. An experienced offensive line blocked and opened holes for what remains one of the school's best running games in history, led by sophomores quarterback Andy Johnson and tail-back Jimmy "the Greek" or "the Greek Streak" Poulos.

The Bulldogs were upset on November 13 in Athens by Auburn and eventual Heisman Trophy recipient Pat Sullivan, and

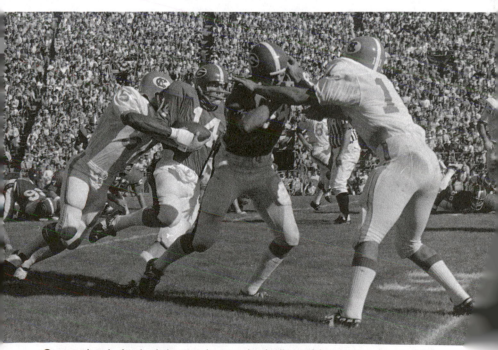

Quarterback Andy Johnson keeps the ball on this play and scrambles for a four-yard gain against North Carolina in the 1971 Gator Bowl.

their SEC and national title aspirations suddenly vanished. After the game, coach Ralph Jordan of Auburn, despite being victorious, declared, "I'm just glad to get out of here. This town is full of maniacs." Following its loss to Auburn, Georgia accepted a December 31 meeting with North Carolina in the Gator Bowl, but its regular-season finale still loomed—a matchup with Georgia Tech on Thanksgiving night.

ABC-TV had instigated the movement of the Georgia–Georgia Tech game from a Saturday to Thanksgiving as the second half of a double-header that featured Nebraska-Oklahoma in the first game, also known as the "Game of the Century." The maneuver created the first nationally televised game in the Georgia–Georgia Tech series and was also the first time the game was played on any day other than Saturday.

The game created a "house divided" for the Robinson and Putnal families. Mixon Robinson was a starting defensive end for Georgia while his brother, Donnie, played on the offensive line for Georgia Tech. Rex Putnal was a receiver at Georgia, while his brother Steve was a defensive lineman for the Yellow Jackets. Mixon and Donnie's father, Joe, humorously said in an interview a couple of days prior to the game, "I've got a red Bulldogs coat and a gold Yellow Jackets one. But I'm thinking I'll probably wear a shrimp-colored one, which is kinda neutral."

The 9–1 and seventh-ranked Bulldogs were eight-point favorites over the Yellow Jackets, who started their year with a 2–4 record before reeling off four consecutive victories. Win or lose, they too would be playing in the postseason, staying in Atlanta for the Peach Bowl. A crowd of 60,124 packed Grant Field, while millions tuned in on their televisions for the nighttime kickoff of the 66th meeting between the intrastate rivals.

Midway through the second quarter, the underdog Yellow Jackets led 14–0 on an Eddie McAshan touchdown pass and a scoring run by Rob Healey. Later, Georgia's Andy Johnson scored on a short run, Cam Bonifay of Georgia Tech kicked a long field goal, and Johnson threw a 23-yard touchdown to Jimmy Shirer just before halftime. Tech led 17–14.

In the third quarter, Johnson scored his second touchdown from a yard out, and Georgia was leading for the first time. Georgia Tech recaptured the lead 24–21 with 10:30 remaining in the game following a 10-yard touchdown run by Healey. With only 3:38 left, Johnson was stopped on fourth down and one from the Yellow Jackets' 9-yard line. It appeared that Georgia Tech was destined to defeat the Bulldogs for the third-consecutive year after Georgia had won five in a row from 1964 to 1968.

Down by three, the Bulldogs' defense forced Tech to punt, surrendering the ball to Georgia on its own 35-yard line with only 1:29 remaining. "In the huddle, everybody was just saying, 'Let's score,'" said Johnson following the game. "I knew we could do it if we wanted to."

After an incomplete pass, Johnson scrambled for 22 yards to the Yellow Jackets' 43-yard line. Johnson failed to connect on three straight passes and faced fourth down and 10 with 57 seconds left. With the game on the line, Johnson then hooked up with tight end Mike Greene for 18 yards and a critical first down.

Two passes were completed to Lynn Hunnicutt for a combined 16 yards, however Johnson was dropped for a four-yard loss back to the 13-yard line with just 28 seconds remaining. Georgia called its final timeout, which was curiously questioned by Georgia Tech head coach Bud Carson the next day as to whether the Bulldogs actually had one to spend.

As Georgia kicker Kim Braswell warmed up in case the Bulldogs were forced to settle for an attempt at a tie, Johnson completed a pass to Jimmy Shirer just inside the 1-yard line. Shirer stepped out of bounds, and the clock stopped with 18 seconds remaining. Georgia head coach Vince Dooley would say after the game that he likely would have kicked a field goal for a tie if his Bulldogs had not driven so close to Tech's goal line.

Lead 44 Right was the play called, and it resulted in Poulos hurdling the pile and barely crossing the goal line for a touchdown. "I was too tired to try it myself," Johnson said afterward. Georgia won the game 28–24 and achieved its first 10-win regular season in 25 years.

Sophomores Poulos and Johnson were spectacular in the historic win. The Greek Streak rushed for 152 yards on 19 carries, while Johnson was responsible for 206 offensive yards (107 passing, 99 rushing), 64 of which were gained on one of the most memorable drives in Bulldogs history.

Dooley vs. Dooley

Coach Vince Dooley's younger brother, Bill, was a top assistant at Georgia during Vince's first three seasons (1964–1966) in Athens. Bill played guard at Mississippi State from 1954 to 1955 and, like brother Vince, was a standout player in the SEC. After three seasons at Georgia, Bill accepted the head coaching position at North Carolina in 1967. The Tar Heels struggled from 1967 to 1969, compiling a 10–20 record, but rebounded to win eight games in 1970 and followed with a 9–2 campaign in '71 for the school's first outright football conference championship since 1949.

A week prior to Georgia defeating Georgia Tech, both Vince's Bulldogs and Bill's Tar Heels accepted a bid from the Gator Bowl in Jacksonville, Florida. They would be making college football history by being the first brothers to face off as head coaches in a bowl game.

A few days prior to the Gator Bowl, Vince commented that in some ways he was looking forward to coaching against his brother, but in other ways he was not. Bill was cautious as his Tar Heels prepared for the Bulldogs, inspecting North Carolina's security to make sure no one could see inside its practice field's fences. A reporter asked Bill, "Surely, you aren't worried about security and spying when you're playing against your brother, are you?" Bill responded, "Well, you just never know."

For the 27th Gator Bowl, 71,208 spectators filled the stadium. North Carolina was seeking its 400th all-time victory, while Georgia was trying to win its first bowl game in four attempts after five years. The first half featured two stellar defenses—the teams combined to punt on 13 occasions and scored no points. Finally, North Carolina's Ken Craven kicked a 35-yard field goal early in the third quarter.

Late in the same quarter, Georgia's Johnson completed a 32-yard pass to Lynn Hunnicutt. On the next play, tailback Poulos broke two tackles and dashed down the sideline for a 25-yard score. Kim Braswell's point after gave the Bulldogs a 7–3 lead late in the third quarter. Georgia's defense held a stagnant Tar Heels offense in check the remainder of the contest, and the Bulldogs prevailed.

After averaging 365 yards, 20 first downs, and 26 points per game during the regular season, North Carolina's offense was held to 181, nine, and three, respectively. Georgia's normally proficient offense also struggled by only gaining 322 total yards—its lowest in more than three months. However, two big plays by Johnson, Hunnicutt, and Poulos had been executed and were just enough to win.

Following the game, defensive coordinator Erk Russell was ceremoniously thrown in the locker room shower by his defenders. Like a good older brother, Vince said that although his Dogs had won, Bill and the Tar Heels had been better prepared. Vince and Bill met only briefly at midfield after the game because of all of the postgame commotion. Not much was said between the brothers as they quickly shook hands and went their separate directions. "I congratulated him on the way his kids played," said Vince. "I was impressed with them, and I'm sure proud of the way Georgia made the plays when it needed, too."

Gimme a Break...or Two

By the end of October 1973, Georgia's record for the season was an uncharacteristic 3–3–1, its worst start after seven games since 1962. This included a 1–3 record in the SEC with losses to Kentucky and Vanderbilt, both of which finished the '73 season with losing records. In the season opener, the Bulldogs settled for a tie against Pittsburgh, a 17-point underdog, who had finished the prior campaign with a 1–10 record. A series of bad breaks played a large part in Georgia's demise. The outlook for the remainder of the schedule looked bleak. The Bulldogs next faced

Tennessee at Neyland Stadium, the SEC's second-best squad behind Alabama and nation's number 11 team, before concluding with Florida, Auburn, and Georgia Tech.

Coach Dooley addressed the Athens Touchdown Club three days before the Tennessee game: "The outlook for the rest of the year is not bright, and I may be underestimating the situation when I say that. But I do feel the team has rededicated themselves to winning."

The Bulldogs believed they could upset Tennessee and were unusually calm prior to battling the Volunteers. "We have a very relaxed team," Dooley would later say. "The night before the Tennessee game, you would have thought they were having a party."

The Bulldogs scored as many touchdowns in their first two possessions against the Volunteers (two) as they had in their previous seven quarters. Unfortunately, Tennessee also scored touchdowns the first two times it touched the football, and the game was tied 14–14 in the second quarter. Following a 37-yard punt return by Georgia's Glynn Harrison, the Dogs added their third touchdown before halftime and led the 11-point favored Volunteers 21–14 at the half.

Tennessee opened the third quarter by scoring 17 straight points and comfortably led 31–21. Later in the final quarter, quarterback Johnson, on a fourth down and two play, completed his only pass of the contest to Poulos for a touchdown. The scoring toss capped a 79-yard drive and pulled the Dogs within three points of the Vols with only 4:27 left in the game.

Tennessee was held on its following possession and lined up to punt from its 28-yard line with approximately three minutes remaining. For whatever reason, although deep in his own territory, Tennessee coach Bill Battle decided to fake the punt. The result of the fake was disastrous for the Volunteers, as Georgia's Dennis Hester tackled upback Steve Chancey for a loss. As the Bulldogs took over on Tennessee's 26-yard line, a showering of boos by Volunteers fans was directed at Battle's play call. Georgia players and coaches had experienced similar ridicule that season in Sanford Stadium.

After four plays, the Bulldogs had gained 18 yards and were only eight yards from the goal line with slightly more than a minute left in the contest. On the next play, Johnson faked to fullback Bobby Burns and attempted to hand it to Harrison, who was expected to run up the middle. Instead, the ball was fumbled but took a perfect bounce off of Tennessee's Tartan Turf into the hands of Johnson. Running around left end, Johnson took the bounced ball into the end zone for a Georgia touchdown. Freshman Allan Leavitt, Georgia's first soccer-style kicker, added his fifth point after of the game. The Bulldogs' defense held the Volunteers on their final drive, and Georgia finally got the breaks in the 35–31 victory.

The Bulldogs' offense rushed for an amazing 356 yards on 77 carries while completing just two passes. At one point in the first half, Georgia executed 43 consecutive running plays before only attempting a pass on a fake field goal. Johnson rushed for 76 yards and a touchdown, threw for a score, and caught a 20-yard pass from tailback King. King rushed for 79 yards and two touchdowns, Poulos finished with 91 rushing yards and was on the receiving end of a scoring pass, and Burns, who generally was a blocking back, rushed 13 times for 74 yards.

Offensive coordinator Frank Inman was given the game ball because his offense generated the most rushing yards against an opponent in more than two seasons. The Bulldogs' stellar rushing performance also prevented the team from losing three games in a row for what would have been only the second time since Dooley's first season. "I've been proud of a lot of teams during my 10 years," said Dooley following the win. "But I've never been prouder of a team than this one. With their backs against the wall, they came up and beat a great Tennessee team."

Boler Was Just Peachy

The Bulldogs of 1973 won three of their final four regular-season games, with a one-point loss to Florida as their only setback. Following a win over Georgia Tech, they accepted a bid to play

18th-ranked Maryland in the sixth-annual Peach Bowl. The Terrapins, coach by Jerry Claiborne, were playing in their first bowl game since 1956 and had been only three points shy of winning an ACC title. Georgia, on the other hand, was playing in its seventh bowl game in the last 10 seasons. With a victory over Maryland, the '73 seniors would depart with 25 wins in three seasons, tying the '68 class for most victories in a three-year span.

Among the Bulldogs playing their last game were standouts quarterback Johnson, tailback Poulos, left guard Mac McWhorter, center Chris Hammond, defensive guard Danny Jones, and safety and punter Don Golden. However, the collegiate career of perhaps Georgia's best player in 1973, linebacker Sylvester Boler, had just recently begun.

Freshman Boler, or the "Black Blur," had suffered two injuries in the first two months of the season and was sidelined for most of the year. Against Tennessee on November 3, Boler took full advantage of the playing time he received as he, according to writer Blake Giles, "tore [Tennessee quarterback] Conredge Holloway's head off." Although Boler played in only half of his first season, some felt he may have been Georgia's greatest line-backer since Vince Dooley's arrival in 1964. The Black Blur combined quickness and a hitting strength matched by very few college linebackers.

While Boler was home in Augusta, Georgia, during Christmas break, he appeared on an Augusta television station singing Christmas carols. As you can imagine, when he returned to Athens for Peach Bowl practices, Boler was the target of amiable joking by his teammates. "I've never heard him sing," said linebackers coach Barry Wilson of the 6'3", 230-pound Boler. "But even if he can't sing, I certainly wouldn't tell him."

Boler and the rest of the Bulldogs would definitely have their hands full against Maryland. It was believed the Terrapins, featuring All-American defensive linemen Randy White and Paul Vellano, may have been the best team Georgia would play all year. This included undefeated Alabama, which would play for the national championship three days following the Peach Bowl.

Trainer and handyman Harry "Squab" Jones, who had been affiliated with Georgia football for more than 50 years, was even somewhat uncertain about the Bulldogs' chances against Maryland. Squab, "as famous among the Georgia people as Gunga Din was with Kipling's readers," according to the 1974 Georgia football media guide, said at the Peach Bowl luncheon two days before the game, "I just can't tell if they are ready to play. I just hope they are ready."

The 1973 Peach Bowl, sponsored by the Lions Clubs of Georgia, kicked off in front of a disappointing 38,107 spectators at Atlanta Stadium. After the initial quarter, the Bulldogs had no first downs and were outgained in yardage 136–7, however the game remained scoreless. Georgia scored the bowl's first points on a screen pass from Johnson to Poulos. After catching the screen, Poulos sidestepped and broke numerous tackles while reversing his field for a spectacular 62-yard touchdown.

Maryland quickly evened the score with trickery from all-purpose star Louis Carter. Tailback Carter was a gifted runner who also had a knack for both receiving and passing the ball. During the regular season, he had completed six of eight passes for five touchdowns. Carter, who was eventually selected as the Peach Bowl's offensive MVP, tossed a 68-yard touchdown to Walter White to put Maryland on the scoreboard. Later in the second quarter, kickers Steve Mike-Mayer and Allan Leavitt traded field goals, and the score was tied 10–10 at halftime.

In the third quarter, Boler forced a Maryland fumble with a bone-crushing tackle, and Georgia recovered on the Terrapins' 8-yard line. Three plays later, Johnson scored from one yard out, and Georgia recaptured the lead with 4:24 remaining in the period.

All Maryland could muster in the second half were two Mike-Mayer field goals as Georgia's defense allowed the Terrapin offense to move up and down the field but never cross its goal line. Boler was voted the game's most outstanding defensive player, and his two forced fumbles, both recovered by Dick Conn, ultimately led to the Bulldogs' 17–16 victory.

Rebuilding Bulldogs

Georgia football's 1974 season was unlike any of the previous 10 coached by Dooley. The offense was explosive and regarded as the Bulldogs' most exciting since the days of Fran Tarkenton. All-SEC selections Randy Johnson and Craig Hertwig spearheaded a veteran offensive line. Harrison and King were one of the best running-back tandems in the country, while quarterback Matt Robinson's play, after beginning the season as the backup signal-caller, was considered the biggest surprise in the SEC.

However, Georgia's defense was unusually inadequate, ranking at or near the bottom in most every defensive category in the conference. After a 17–13 loss to Auburn on November 16, Georgia's record was a substandard 6–4 with two games remaining: Georgia Tech then Miami of Ohio in the Tangerine Bowl.

Despite the fact that Georgia Tech featured a run-oriented wishbone offense while Georgia ranked last in the SEC in defending the run, the Bulldogs were viewed as eight-point favorites to defeat Tech. Only 47,500 spectators were present in Sanford Stadium for the regular-season finale primarily because of a driving rain but also because of Georgia's mediocre showing during the season.

Coach Pepper Rodgers' Yellow Jackets led 20–0 at halftime in the process of dealing Georgia a 34–14 loss. As was the case for most of the season, the Bulldogs could not stop the run, allowing 275 rushing yards and five ball carriers to rush for 32 yards or more. Besides Harrison rushing for 101 yards, Georgia's "explosive" veer offense could never get on track. Robinson was responsible for only one offensive yard in seven plays, while the Bulldogs committed four turnovers and did not complete a single pass.

Miami had not lost in 22 consecutive games dating back to its season finale in 1972, including a 16–7 victory over Florida in the 1973 Tangerine Bowl. The Redskins had a spectacular defense that was allowing fewer than seven points per game during their winning streak. For the 29th Tangerine Bowl in Orlando, Florida, the Bulldogs, a member of one of the best conferences in college football, was inconceivably a two-point underdog to a team from the disregarded Mid-American Conference.

In front of a spectators record Tangerine Bowl crowd of 20,246, Robinson lost a fumble on the first snap of the game. Six plays later, Miami scored and led 7–0 early. Georgia drove 75 yards in 10 plays on its second drive, highlighted by a 43-yard completion from Robinson to Appleby, but had to settle for a 20-yard field goal by Leavitt. The Redskins responded with two quick touchdowns and led 21–3 with 14:18 still remaining in the second quarter.

Miami would not score again in the game, but its three early touchdowns would be enough to defeat Georgia 21–10. Robinson passed for 190 yards while Harrison rushed for 69, but the Dogs would cross Miami's goal line just once on a one-yard run by quarterback Ray Goff for the only score of the second half. The Bulldogs outgained the Redskins in yardage (274–267), but two fumbles inside their own 25-yard line led to Miami touchdowns and Georgia's downfall. It was the lowest point for Georgia football in Dooley's 11 seasons at the helm.

After the defeat, the Georgia players reportedly walked off the Tangerine Bowl field as if they had no concern for what had just transpired. "This is my most disappointing season, especially the way we wound up," said Coach Dooley after the loss. "I think we're in the most critical rebuilding stage we've ever been in. We will have to build from the ground up." Dooley also commented that he was delighted that the 1974 season was over so he could aim for the following year.

chapter 12

Junkyard Dogs

Defensive coordinator Erk Russell, faced with a small and inexperienced unit in 1975, turned his Bulldogs into the Junkyard Dogs.

"Meaner than a Junkyard Dog"

As summer practices began for the 1975 team, the defense was undoubtedly the major focus point and area of concern. Only two starters, Rusty Russell and David Schwak, returned from the inept '74 defensive unit. Russell would be playing a new position, switching from defensive end to linebacker. In addition, as many as seven of the starting 11 defensive positions were unsettled with only three weeks before the first game of the year, against Pittsburgh.

The Bulldogs' offense appeared to be strong with an intact line and backfield from the prior season and possibly the best set of receivers ever at Georgia. However, because of the small and inexperienced defense, the Dogs' preseason predictions were among their lowest in more than 10 years. Of the four players listed on preseason All-SEC squads—Glynn Harrison, Allan Leavitt, Gene Washington, and Randy Johnson—none played on the defensive side of the ball.

The 1975 defense would use the unique split-60 formation, a set not used by any other college team at the time. Faced with a new formation and a group of small defenders, defensive coordinator Erk Russell felt his players needed a moniker to inspire spirit amongst themselves.

Russell's defenders may have been small in stature, inexperienced, and given little chance to succeed, but they were quick and feisty like junkyard dogs. The term "junkyard dog" had first been widely broadcast two years before in Jim Croce's song "Bad, Bad Leroy Brown," where Leroy is "badder than old King Kong and meaner than a junkyard dog."

"There isn't anything meaner than a junkyard dog," said Russell in mid-August of 1975. "They aren't good for nothing except for being mean and ornery. That's what we want our defense to be."

In an interview with the *Athens Banner-Herald*, assistant coach John Kasay spoke of some well-known junkyard dogs in Athens apart from the ones on the football team. He told of two that guarded Parrish Toyota, one at University Chevrolet, and the junkyard dog at Carter's Carburetor that was half blind, underfed, and ferocious at night. A few days before the season opener, enthusiasm for Georgia's defense was rampant in the town and at the university. Junkyard Dogs T-shirts were popular clothing items in the Athens area.

The Junkyard Dogs played admirably against Pittsburgh, holding the Panthers to 266 total yards in the contest and the heralded All-American Tony Dorsett to 17 rushing yards in the first half. However, the undersized defense wore down in the final quarter and surrendered 13 points, while Georgia's offense was ineffective in a 19–9 loss. In a losing effort, the Junkyard Dogs penetrated the line well, usually seemed to be in the right place at the right time, and appeared a step quicker than 1974's unit.

The Bulldogs, written off and selected toward the bottom of the conference in August, won five of their next six games and were 5–2 in late October with games against Richmond, Florida, Auburn, and Georgia Tech remaining. Much of the unexpected success was because of the Junkyard Dogs' defense, which was allowing only 287 yards and fewer than 14 points per game after yielding 357 yards and 24 points per contest in 1974.

Dooley's Junkyard Dogs

Following a Georgia victory in September 1975 and an impressive performance by the defense, University of Georgia football network announcer Happy Howard paid tribute to the Junkyard Dogs. Early in the football season, Howard spent three weeks writing the song, "Dooley's Junkyard Dogs." James Brown, the Godfather of Soul, was from Augusta, Georgia, and a big Bulldogs fan and was asked if he would sing and record the tune. "Dooley's Junkyard Dogs" was cut in October with approximately 100,000 records released shortly thereafter.

Howard said that he wrote the song because Georgia's defensive play was so surprising and deserved some notoriety. The tune took 14 hours to cut, with about 35 musicians and singers, including Brown, working on the recording. As Georgia prepared for its final four games of the regular season, a press conference was held on October 29 at Atlanta's International Motel with Howard, Brown, and Coach Dooley announcing the release of "Dooley's Junkyard Dogs."

What began as the Georgia defense's moniker and inspiration for the 1975 season is still remembered more than 30 years later. At Georgia football tailgates even today, you can still hear fans playing and singing Brown's song. Interestingly, the original song referred to certain players' names from the '75 team, which you will not hear mentioned in the most recent rendition. The following is an excerpt from the original version:

There's Swoopes, Clark, Rusty, and Zambiasi
But they'll hit you, man, and make you dizzy
There's Wilson, Johnson, and some dude named Moon Pie
There's Henderson, Appleby, and that character named Miller
Even greater than the thriller in Manila
Dooley's Junkyard Dogs
Dooley's Junkyard Dogs

Goff Shoestrings Vandy

On October 11, 1975, the Bulldogs were upset by Ole Miss 28–13 in Georgia's first ever visit to Oxford, Mississippi. The following week, the Dogs traveled to Nashville, Tennessee, with a 3–2 record and desperate for a win. Seemingly, a victory was not going to be easy. Georgia was missing several key players to injuries, including running back Glynn Harrison and kicker Allan Leavitt.

In pouring rain and on a soggy surface at Dudley Field, the Commodores jumped out to a 3–0 lead following a field goal. Georgia retaliated in the second quarter on a two-yard touchdown run by Andy Reid. Midway through the second quarter and with the Bulldogs leading 7–3, Lawrence Craft recovered a Vanderbilt fumble on the host's 36-yard line. On the next snap, quarterback Ray Goff was stopped for no gain on first down. What followed

Gene Washington (82) was on the receiving end of one of the more famous plays in Georgia history, the Shoestring Play that resulted in Washington's touchdown against a stunned Vanderbilt defense in 1975.

next was Georgia executing one of the most unusual plays in college football history.

With the ball spotted on the right hash mark, Goff walked up to the ball, knelt, and pretended to tie his shoe. Meanwhile, the rest of the Georgia offense stood nonchalantly near the left hash. Goff suddenly and legally pitched the football to flanker Gene Washington, who took off running down the sideline. As most of Vanderbilt's defense stood bewildered, Washington sprinted 36 yards with plenty of blocking for a touchdown.

Georgia had run the Shoestring Play, chicanery which usually occurred in backyard and sandlot football. Offensive line coach Jimmy Vickers had suggested the play to Dooley four days prior to the game. While watching game film, Vickers had noticed that players in Vanderbilt's defensive huddle would often turn their backs on offenses while calling the defense's signals. An inattentive defense like Vanderbilt's could be vulnerable to "shoestring" deception.

Washington said later that he had a hard time keeping a grin off of his face just prior to Georgia running the play. Most of the Commodore's defensive unit had their backs turned as Goff shoveled the ball to the speedster, and "there was nothing to it after that," according to Washington. Vanderbilt head coach Fred Pancoast, Georgia's offensive coordinator during the 1970 and 1971 seasons, said that the shoestring was "the big play of the game. I thought we lost our poise after that."

The Bulldogs would score 33 more points in an eventual 47–3 victory over the Commodores: Hilton Young scored on two rushes, Al Pollard ran for a touchdown, Matt Robinson threw a five-yard scoring pass to Steve Davis, and backup kicker Cary Long booted Georgia's first two field goals of the season. Eleven Bulldog ball carriers combined to rush for 297 yards. Kevin McLee led the way with 90 rushing yards on 18 carries. The Junkyard Dogs held the Commodores to 151 total yards, the defense's best outing since allowing only 142 yards to Auburn in 1973.

Young was a remarkable story in his own right. The 5'7" running back from Athens was a former scout team player and only played against Vanderbilt because of the injury to Harrison. In just his second appearance on Georgia's varsity squad, Young carried the ball eight times and scored touchdowns on one- and two-yard runs. He had rarely traveled with the team on away games and, along with kicker Long, flew on a plane for the first time in his life for the Vanderbilt contest.

End Around and Defense Downs Gators

During 1975's Homecoming game, Georgia was on the verge of losing to Richmond before rallying for a 28–24 win. A loss by the Bulldogs to the Spiders would have been one of the most devastating defeats in Georgia football history. Regardless, the Bulldogs' record was 6–2 after the fortunate victory. Georgia was now ready to make its annual trek to Jacksonville for the World's Largest Outdoor Cocktail Party.

The Gators of '75 were regarded as perhaps the best team ever at Florida. Although ranked 11th nationally, Florida was considered to have top-five or better talent and was in strong contention to win its first conference title in its 70-year history. The

7–1 Gators were averaging 335 yards rushing per game and 100 more passing from the wishbone formation. Florida's defense was equally impressive, allowing only nine and a half points and forcing nearly four turnovers per game from its opponents. Even the Gators' coach, Doug Dickey, had recently been discussing how formidable his squad was. A week before the Florida game, Coach Dooley was quoted as saying, "Realistically, it's a mighty long shot for us [to win]." The spread-setters in Las Vegas agreed and made Georgia a substantial underdog of 10½ points.

A Gator Bowl crowd of 71,416 witnessed Georgia lose a fumble on its initial drive. After the ball was recovered, the Gators drove for a touchdown by Tony Green on a one-yard run with 8:22 remaining in the opening frame. Before the half, Georgia gained 22 yards on consecutive plays: a pass from Goff to Washington and a run by Harrison. However, the Bulldogs had to settle for a 21-yard field goal by Leavitt seconds before halftime.

Similar to most of the first half, a defensive battle characterized the third and fourth quarters. With 3:42 remaining in the game, Georgia faced a four-point deficit and had the ball on its own 20-yard line. Florida, on the other hand, was fewer than four minutes away from likely winning at least a share of its first SEC championship.

Quarterback Matt Robinson handed the ball to tight end Richard Appleby, running an end around from his left to the right. Appleby had already run two end arounds that day, gaining a combined 30 yards. However, this time, instead of running, Appleby planted his feet and flung the football 45 yards downfield. Washington caught the pass in stride at Florida's 35-yard line and waltzed into the end zone. After the game, Appleby said, "Man, when I saw Gene clear that Florida cornerback, I knew it was going to work." Leavitt's point after was good, and Georgia led 10–7.

Florida would still have two opportunities to win the ballgame. After the Appleby-to-Washington wonder, the Gators drove into Georgia's territory. However, defensive end Dicky Clark forced a fumble from quarterback Don Gaffney that was recovered by Georgia's Schwak.

With 1:42 remaining in the game, the Gators drove to Georgia's 21-yard line. In scoring position, Gaffney threw three straight incomplete passes, and Florida faced fourth down and 10 with 50 seconds remaining. Everyone in the Gator Bowl was surprised when Coach Dickey decided to try a game-tying field goal. Florida's snapper, Leroy Cline, had not warmed up for a field-goal attempt because he never thought his coach would settle for a tie game. Dickey would say later that he believed a tie with Georgia would still give Florida a good chance to eventually win the SEC title.

Nevertheless, the Gators' field-goal attempt never got off the ground. Cline's snap was poor, throwing off the timing of kicker David Posey. Posey's missed attempt merely dribbled into the line. Georgia won 10–7 in spectacular fashion.

Although the Junkyard Dogs allowed Florida 20 first downs and 382 total yards, the defense stopped the Gators on third- and fourth-down situations several times. Appleby's touchdown pass to Washington might have scored Georgia's game-winning touchdown, but it was the Junkyard Dogs' defense that defeated Florida. "The defense carried us all day," said Coach Dooley after the game. "Our defense has determined how Georgia has done all year."

Awesome Atmosphere for Alabama in '76

Georgia finished the 1975 season with a 9–3 record, surprising all of college football and probably even itself. Expectations were high in 1976, as many preseason prognosticators indicated the Bulldogs would challenge Alabama for the SEC crown. The Crimson Tide had captured five consecutive conference titles, and there was no reason to believe they could not win a sixth.

During the preseason, members of the Georgia offense shaved their heads to signify unity, and the Junkyard Dogs were now known as "the Runts." Defensive coordinator Russell changed the name of his small but determined defenders despite some objection. "It sounds kind of downgrading to me," said cornerback Bobby Thompson. "I'd prefer Junkyard Dogs II or something."

Also that summer, the team was dealt a devastating blow when Hugh Hendrix, the starting left guard in '75, died from a rare blood infection. The Bulldogs would dedicate their season to their deceased teammate.

Georgia began the year with three wins and climbed to number six in the Associated Press rankings by the end of September. Next on the schedule was Alabama, coached by Bear Bryant. The Crimson Tide had stunningly lost to Ole Miss in the season opener but was ranked 10th in the nation and was nearly a touchdown favorite over Georgia.

The atmosphere in Athens and around Sanford Stadium for the Georgia-Alabama game has been described as unparalleled. Tickets to the game were being scalped for as much as $100 each, which was a significant amount of money for a ticket to a football game more than 30 years ago.

A number of Georgia followers would assemble on the railroad tracks outside Sanford Stadium for every home game to view games free of charge. These "track fans" began arriving the day before and spent the night in sleeping bags to assure themselves a spot on the tracks. On the day of the game, the fans had taken up every inch of space on and around the tracks by 10:00 that morning. "We went to the stadium to practice at 3:30 Friday afternoon, and people were already on the tracks," said Alabama guard Doug Collins. "Those people were ready for that game." Reportedly, one track fan spotted a friend amongst the railroad crowd and hollered, "How long you been here?" The friend said, wavering, "About two quarts of vodka!"

Writer Ron Hudspeth visited the university's main library to see if he could possibly find anyone studying and missing one of the greatest events and parties ever in Athens. Much to his amazement, he did find a few, including a female graduate student who said, "I sort of compare what's going on here this week to the Bicentennial.... It's everywhere—on the radio, TV, the billboards. I've had it. I think I hate Red and Black." She and a few thousand Alabama fans were likely the only ones in Athens that day to feel that way.

The first half of the game was scoreless until Georgia's Robinson capped a 14-play, 67-yard drive with a three-yard touchdown run just before halftime. The Bulldogs would score twice in the second half on a Rayfield Williams two-yard run and a pass from Robinson to Ulysses Norris. Alabama's feared wishbone offense that also showcased a great passing game was shut out for the first time since Coach Bryant first decided to run the wishbone in 1971.

In their 21–0 victory, the Bulldogs rushed for 190 yards against the SEC's top rushing defense while holding the conference's best rushing offense to 49 rushing yards on 45 carries. Alabama quarterback Jeff Rutledge rushed for a net loss of 55 yards, including being sacked six times in the final quarter.

In what was called the biggest game for Georgia since Auburn in 1971 and the loudest affair in Athens since Auburn visited in 1959, Alabama's loss eliminated any chance for a sixth-consecutive SEC title. On the other hand, Georgia's notable victory gave the Bulldogs a legitimate opportunity for their first conference championship in eight seasons.

Fourth and Dumb

Georgia and Florida entered their matchup in 1976 with only one loss apiece and, for the first time, the teams faced one another when each was ranked in the Associated Press's top 10. As was the case for the past few seasons, Florida had an explosive offense, averaging 30 points and 421 yards per game. Earlier in the week of the game, defensive coordinator Russell indicated that the Bulldogs could use a 12th man to stop the Gator offense.

Bulldogs' quarterback Goff ran and passed for scores prior to halftime, but Georgia's defense allowed 27 first-half points. The Dogs suffered several defensive breakdowns and made critical mistakes in allowing the most points in any half since yielding 28 first-half points to South Carolina in 1970.

Losing 27–14 early in the third quarter, Georgia drove 81 yards in seven plays and scored on a six-yard pass from Goff to Norris. The Gators got the ball and picked up nine yards in three plays. Facing fourth down and two feet from its own 29-yard line, Florida elected not to punt with a little more than eight minutes remaining in the third quarter while holding a seven-point advantage. Instead, the usually conservative Coach Dickey of Florida decided to gamble and go for the first down.

Fullback Earl Carr of Florida took a pitch outside from quarterback Jimmy Fisher. Reading the play perfectly, Georgia defensive back John Henderson dropped Carr for no gain, and the Bulldogs took over on the Gators' 29-yard line, down only 27–20. In an attempt to gain momentum, Coach Dickey had given Georgia the upper hand with his risky decision. Carr even questioned his own coach in a comment he made following the game: "When I was running the play, I was asking myself why in the world we were running this play."

Six plays after the failed fourth-down conversion, Georgia's Al Pollard scored on a two-yard run, and Leavitt's point after tied the score. In the final quarter, Goff rushed for two touchdowns while Florida was held scoreless, and the Bulldogs defeated the Gators 41–27. Goff was named ABC-TV's top offensive player, despite a 198-yard rushing effort by teammate Kevin McLee. Goff completed five of five passes for 37 yards, rushed for 124 yards on 17 carries, and was responsible for five touchdowns. In addition, Pollard gained 84 rushing yards as Georgia rushed 79 times for 432 yards, single-game totals that rank third- and fifth-most in the school history even today.

The Bulldogs' defense was unyielding in the second half. After allowing 27 points and 234 total yards in the first half, Georgia shut out Florida while allowing only 65 yards in the final two quarters. The momentum the Dogs gained after stopping the Gators on the fourth-down play was partly responsible for their outstanding second-half performance. The next day, a Jacksonville newspaper article covering the game was titled "Fourth and Dumb," in regard to Dickey's decision.

For the second year in a row, Georgia knocked Florida out of SEC title contention. Following the game, Dickey said the Florida coaching staff "did a miserable job in the second half.... I made some dumb calls."

Jubilant Bulldogs fans streamed onto the Gator Bowl field after the victory and tore down both goalposts. As a Georgia player attempted to wade through the crowd, he remarked that it was easy for the Bulldogs to get through the Florida defense in the second half, but reaching the dressing room after the game was a different story.

chapter 13

Wonderdogs and the Most Wonderful Recruit

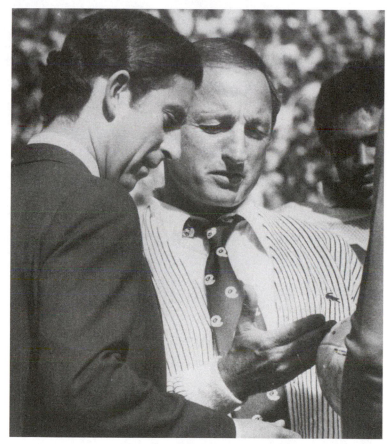

Prince Charles was on hand for the Kentucky game in 1977, but unfortunately the Wildcats handed the Dawgs their worst regular-season defeat in 15 seasons. Photo courtesy of the UGA Sports Information Department.

Royalty Backs the Bulldogs

The Dogs followed an SEC championship and Sugar Bowl berth in 1976 by recording their only losing campaign in Coach Vince Dooley's 25 seasons at Georgia. The 1977 team was plagued by injuries and fumbling, as a school-record 35 fumbles were lost during the year. In Georgia's last game against Georgia Tech, fourth-string quarterback Randy Cook started the game but was injured. Freshman Chris Welton followed but was also soon forced out with an injury. Georgia ended its season forced to use Davey Sawyer, a sixth-string quarterback who had played just two days earlier in the Georgia–Georgia Tech freshman game.

One of the few highlights of the 1977 season was the ceremonies during a halftime show honoring the attendance of Charles Philip Arthur George Windsor-Mountbatten, the Prince of Wales. Prince Charles had been touring various parts of the United States. After visiting Charleston, South Carolina, on the morning of October 22, he flew into Athens in time for the Georgia-Kentucky halftime ceremonies. As he arrived at Sanford Stadium for his first American football game, Prince Charles became the first member of Great Britain's Royal Family to attend a college football game since Queen Elizabeth witnessed Maryland–North Carolina in 1957.

As the prince walked onto the field at halftime, much of the sold-out crowd of 59,100 chanted "damn good prince," similar to how "damn good dog" is cheered for their mascot Uga. The prince joined coaches Dooley and Fran Curci and captains Jeff Lewis of Georgia and Kentucky's Art Still. Prince Charles was given a signed football from Dooley that read: "To HRH (His Royal Highness) Prince Charles, from Georgia, 1976 SEC Champions."

As he was walking off the field, the 28-year-old prince stopped to talk with two female members of Georgia's band and asked one if she was a drum major. After the majorette said she was a solo twirler, he inquired what that was and indicated he had enjoyed the show. James Brown also performed at halftime, singing and dancing to "Dooley's Junkyard Dogs."

During the third quarter, Prince Charles sat in the university president's private box with president Fred Davison and Governor George Busbee and, according to writer Tom Crawford, "saw the Georgia team take a worse beating than the British took from the American revolutionaries 200 years ago."

The Bulldogs suffered their worst regular-season defeat since 1962. The eighth-ranked Wildcats held Georgia to only eight first downs while yielding 127 total yards during their 33–0 victory.

When asked after the game about his visit with Prince Charles, Dooley related: "He said, 'Since you're behind, I guess I better pull for you?' And I told him we needed it."

Underdogs No More

Georgia's prognosis for the 1978 season was seemingly similar to what had transpired the year before—a losing campaign. Eight of 11 starters had departed from the '77 defense, including All-Americans Bill Krug and Ben Zambiasi and All-SEC selection Ronnie Swoopes. The only returning Bulldog receiving any kind of star billing was tailback Willie McClendon. He and the rest of the Georgia offense would be running the I formation in an effort to minimize the fumbles to which the Bulldogs had been susceptible when using the veer offensive scheme.

One particular forecaster predicted that Georgia's October 21 meeting with Vanderbilt would decide who would finish last in the SEC. Many preseason predictions indicated the Bulldogs' only assured victory was a November 4 date with the Virginia Military Institute—a current Division I-AA team. As the rebuilding 1978 season began, the team would not be known as Junkyard Dogs or Runts, but as the "Underdogs," according to defensive coordinator Russell.

It had been a rare occurrence for Georgia to be an under-dog at home in Sanford Stadium. However, the Bulldogs opened the season hosting Baylor then Clemson and were underdogs for both contests. Georgia followed a 16–14 upset win over Baylor by shutting out Clemson 12–0 and reaching number 19 in the Associated Press rankings. The Tigers would eventually capture an ACC championship and finish with an 11–1 record in 1978, their lone setback coming against Georgia. After a loss to South Carolina, Georgia improved its record to 3–1 with a 39-point blowout victory over Ole Miss. It soon became apparent the so-called preseason experts were mistaken.

For the fourth time in five games, Georgia was again an underdog when it met Louisiana State in Baton Rouge. LSU's Charles Alexander, who had rushed for 156 yards on 40 carries the week before against Florida, was the top rusher in the SEC. Georgia's McClendon was directly behind him, ranking second in the conference.

It was the first time the Bulldogs had played in LSU's raucous "Death Valley" in 26 years. Tiger Stadium at night has a gameday atmosphere like no other school's, where there is "only" a problem, according to a stadium security guard, "when someone starts throwing bottles off the top of the stands."

Alexander rushed for a three-yard touchdown following a fumble by Georgia's Scott Woerner while fielding a punt. LSU seemed on its way to a one-sided win after an 82-yard scoring pass from Steve Ensminger to Carlos Carson. It was the first play off the Tigers bench for Ensminger, who would later become Georgia's quarterback coach from 1991 to 1993. The Bulldogs would reduce LSU's lead to 14–7 following a 24-yard touchdown run by McClendon. Later, Mike Conway's 39-yard field goal gave the Tigers a 17–7 halftime lead.

In what Coach Dooley later described as a "weird" game, Georgia scored 17 unanswered points in the third quarter. The second half began with an electrifying 99-yard kickoff return for a touchdown by receiver Lindsay Scott. On Scott's return, the freshman appeared as if he would go out of bounds near LSU's 20-yard line, but kept his balance and made it into the end zone. The return also broke a school record set by Lamar Davis, who returned a kick 96 yards against Tulane for a score in 1940. Following a Woerner interception, Rex Robinson tied the contest with a 29-yard field goal.

Late in the third quarter, Georgia's Gordon Terry forced a fumble recovered by Tim Parks on the LSU 40-yard line. A few plays later, McClendon's six-yard touchdown and Robinson's point after gave Georgia a 24–17 edge with 59 seconds remaining in the quarter.

The Tigers tried to mount a final drive during the last 1:03 of the game. A David Woodley incomplete pass was followed with a long bomb dropped by Carson that likely would have been the tying touchdown. After Woodley completed a seven-yard pass, LSU faced fourth down and 3 on its own 22-yard line. Inexplicably, Woodley threw his next pass out of bounds to kill the clock, apparently forgetting that it was fourth down.

In Georgia's third upset victory of the season, McClendon (27 rushes, 144 yards, two touchdowns) outperformed Alexander (22 rushes, 81 yards, one touchdown). The Bulldogs' defense held the ninth-best offense in the nation scoreless in the last half and snapped Alexander's eight-game, 100-yard rushing streak, while linebacker Ricky McBride set a modern Georgia record with 24 tackles (18 solo, six assists).

"We have been an underdog pulling upsets," said Dooley after the win. "Now we won't be an underdog. The question is: are we good enough to play as the favorites?"

Young Belue to the Rescue

The 1978 Dogs would be labeled the "Wonderdogs" for their comeback victories and wins over favored opposition. They upset Baylor, Clemson, and LSU, rallied to defeat Kentucky and tie Auburn, and squeezed past Florida by two points. As Georgia hosted bowl-bound Georgia Tech in the final game of the regular season, the Bulldogs were 8–1–1 and ranked 11th in the Associated Press poll, eighth in the United Press International.

The Yellow Jackets appeared in the process of wrecking the Wonderdogs, leading 20–0 in the second quarter. Three lost fumbles by Georgia led to a Georgia Tech touchdown and two field goals. The Yellow Jackets also recovered an onside kick, which led to a one-yard scoring run by Rodney Lee. With 4:38 remaining until halftime, struggling Georgia quarterback Jeff Pyburn was benched for freshman Buck Belue.

Having played only sparingly all season, Belue had completed just seven of 19 passes with three interceptions. Regardless, offensive coordinator Bill Pace suggested the switch for the freshman, which immediately paid off. Belue later commented on being summoned into action for Pyburn: "I wasn't nervous at all.... I knew I had to make something happen." Belue promptly drove the Bulldogs 55 yards to a one-yard touchdown run by McClendon. Georgia trailed 20–7 at the half.

In the third quarter, McClendon scored his second touchdown following an interception by Woerner, who was chosen the most outstanding defensive player of the game. Later, Woerner scored on an electrifying 72-yard punt return. Rex Robinson's point after was converted, and Georgia rallied to claim a 21–20 advantage. The Bulldogs' lead was short-lived, however, as Georgia Tech's Drew Hill returned the ensuing kickoff 100 yards for a touchdown. The Yellow Jackets converted a two-point attempt and jumped ahead 28–21.

Late in the game, Belue engineered a nine-play, 84-yard drive, twice converting fourth downs. The last conversion was from Georgia Tech's 42-yard line as Georgia faced fourth and three. Belue rolled to his right and almost decided to run for the first down until he was surrounded by a couple of Yellow Jackets. As he was being tackled, Belue flung a pass downfield to a wide-open Amp Arnold, who caught the ball around Georgia Tech's 20-yard line. Arnold coasted into the end zone for a touchdown with only 2:24 remaining in the game. It was supposed to have been only a five- or six-yard out pattern for Arnold, but it turned out to be a touchdown covering 42 yards. After the game, Belue described the play: "I saw Amp standing out there all alone and just tossed it to him."

Instead of kicking the extra point, Georgia decided to go for two points and the lead. On the first attempt, Belue's pass was incomplete, but tight end Mark Hodge was interfered, so Georgia was given another chance. On the second attempt, Belue faked the ball to McClendon, began to run toward his left, and at the last moment pitched it to a trailing Arnold, who ran untouched into the end zone for the conversion. Georgia had recaptured the lead 29–28.

Georgia Tech was not finished, however, as quarterback Mike Kelly moved the Yellow Jackets 54 yards in four plays from their own 9-yard line. With just over a minute to play in the contest, Georgia Tech was on the Bulldogs' 37-yard line and only needed a field goal for victory. Kelly dropped back to pass again but was intercepted by freshman David Archer on the 27-yard line. The rarely used Archer was in the game for his first play and did not even have his name on the back of his jersey like most every other Bulldog player.

In just over two quarters of work, Belue completed seven of nine passes for 90 yards, including the touchdown to Arnold. He also was third on the team in rushing, with 19 yards on 10 carries. Most importantly, the freshman rallied the Bulldogs from a 20-point deficit for their sixth comeback victory of the season in true Wonderdog fashion.

The Hunt for Herschel

The Bulldogs ended their 1978 campaign in a manner that contradicted how they played during the regular season. In the Bluebonnet Bowl, Georgia led innovative coach Bill Walsh and his Stanford Cardinals 22–0 in the third quarter, and it appeared the Bulldogs were well on their way to their second 10-win season in three years. However, Stanford rallied to score three touchdowns in fewer than five minutes in the third quarter and eventually kicked a field goal in the final quarter to defeat the Wonderdogs 25–22.

Georgia's misfortune continued into the following year, as the Bulldogs dropped their first three games by a total of 13 points. However, Georgia responded to its dismal start by winning six of its eight final games and nearly winning an SEC title and earning a trip to the Sugar Bowl with a 6–5 record.

Overall, the 1979 Bulldogs were a talented squad. They had a good defense that forced more turnovers that season than any other team in the nation. In addition, Georgia's passing game was adequate and its special teams were admirable. Early in the '79 season, however, the Bulldogs' luck seemed to run out, and, throughout the year, the offense lacked a consistent running game.

Like most leading football programs in the country, Georgia desperately recruited a particular running back for its 1980 freshman class: Herschel Walker from Wrightsville, Georgia. At Johnson County High School Walker rushed for a remarkable 6,137 career yards, averaged 7.8 yards per carry, and scored 86 touchdowns. Georgia was one of many schools that ventured to Wrightsville on a regular basis to pursue the heralded Walker. According to author Bill Cromartie, Dooley appointed Georgia assistant coach Mike Cavan to be vice president in charge of Herschel. Cavan spent so much of his time in Wrightsville recruiting Walker that he should have been forced to pay taxes.

February's national letter of intent signing date for college football recruits came and went in 1980, and Walker still had not signed with a school. Herschel seemed to be delaying his signing, for whatever reason, and the postponement was taking its toll on the Walker family.

Herschel's mother, Christine, was sick and tired of all the recruiters coming by the house, the numerous phone calls, and her son's delay. "Why don't you make up your mind?" she asked Herschel. "Make a decision! Don't you ever get tired of having to meet with all these people?"

By late March, Walker still had not made his decision. However, he had indicated to his high school coach, Gary Phillips, that he had narrowed his choices to Clemson, Southern Cal, UCLA, Georgia Tech, and Georgia.

It's Heads! Georgia Wins the Toss!

On Easter morning of 1980, Walker told his mother he was going to make a decision on where he was going to play college foot-

Georgia ultimately won the Herschel Walker derby, and, despite Coach Dooley's reservations, the freshman made an impact of monstrous proportions.

ball. However, instead of stating which school he would attend, he cut up scraps of paper and asked his mother to write "Alabama," "Clemson," "USC," and "Georgia" on each piece. Walker then dropped the scraps into a paper bag and shook the bag. Mother and son agreed that the first school selected three times would be where he would attend. Christine Walker later said that Herschel "picked Georgia more times than any of the other three." Christine also suggested that a coin be flipped. "If the coin turned up heads," she said, "that would be the lucky school.... So we did that—and every time it came out Georgia!"

Walker had finally decided to attend and play football at the University of Georgia. Christine telephoned Herschel's high school coach, who notified Georgia assistant Cavan. Phillips later indicated that Walker did not decide right away where he would attend school because he had a "really hard time saying no to people." Cavan had been instrumental in the recruitment of Walker and, at the time of Walker's decision, was participating in an Easter egg hunt in Lawrenceville, Georgia. When Cavan was told of Herschel's decision, according to author Jeff Prugh, "he let out a wild, delirious scream. His family thought he'd been shot."

As Walker prepared to make it official that he would attend Georgia, people began arriving at the Walker home to witness his signing. Included was Freddy Jones, a writer for the *Macon Telegraph,* who was hurrying toward the house in his car but was pulled over by a state patrolman for speeding. Jones tried to explain to the officer he was only speeding to observe the signing of Herschel Walker. "Where's he goin' to school?" the patrolman asked. "Georgia," answered Jones. "All right! You go on ahead," the jubilant officer said without writing Jones a speeding ticket.

Another writer, Doug Hall of the Dublin *Courier Herald*, apparently later asked Walker why it took so long for him to make a decision. He recalled, "Herschel looked at me and said, 'I knew what I was gonna do all along.'" Seemingly, it helped Georgia's cause that Southern Cal was headed for an apparent probation because of a junior college transcript scandal.

After signing with Georgia, Walker told an *Atlanta Constitution* writer, "I felt real nice at Georgia. And I didn't want to go too far from home. I wanted my family to be able to come and see me play. It's only about 94 miles from my house to Athens."

Several months before the beginning of the 1980 season, Dooley said that he did not expect Walker as a freshman to be the main tailback for Georgia. For one, Walker had played in only Class A high school football, where, according to Dooley, "the schools are smaller and the players are smaller." Dooley added, "I really don't see him giving us a whole lot of help next year."

chapter 14

Undefeated, Untied, and Consensus National Champions

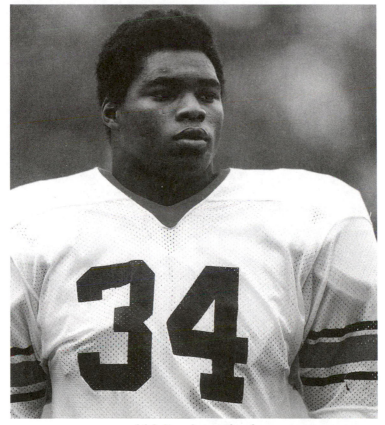

Walker's arrival on campus was somewhat overwhelming to both the freshman and the fans, but once he took the field he was every bit in charge. Photo courtesy of Getty Images.

Here's Herschel...

On August 16, 1980, Georgia held its annual Picture Day, attended by the largest crowd in recent memory. Besides the long lines, autographs, and photographs, Coach Vince Dooley unveiled the new pants his squad would be sporting for the 1980 season— silver britches. Georgia had worn silver pants during the Wally Butts and Johnny Griffith eras. Once Dooley arrived in 1964, the silver britches were retired and white pants, and occasionally red ones in the late 1970s, were worn by the Bulldogs. Now, new silver britches were being unveiled at Georgia's Woodruff Field, the team's practice field, in front of approximately 2,000 fans.

Leroy Dukes, a member of the last Georgia team to wear silver britches, was present passing out hats that declared, "Go You Silver Britches." Bumper stickers were also distributed with the same slogan.

The afternoon's main attraction was the freshman Herschel Walker, who had yet to play a single down of college football. "I sure wasn't expecting this," Walker said of Picture Day. "But I'm having a good time, even though I've never held so many babies in my life."

After a particular young boy got Walker's autograph, he prophesied, "He's the greatest football player in the country, and he's going to make Georgia the best football team in the country." It was a lofty prediction for an 18-year old freshman, especially one whose coach had indicated would not play a major role for the 1980 team. "I just wanted to make the traveling squad," Walker would say later. "I just wanted to get some experience." As it turned out, he would do much more than that.

There Goes Herschel...

As Georgia's opening game of the 1980 season against Tennessee approached, every one of the 24 starters seemed certain, except who would start at tailback. It had been a wide-open race from the beginning as senior Donnie McMickens, sophomore Carnie Norris, junior Matt Simon, and true freshmen Walker and Barry Young contended for the starting tailback position.

The Monday before the Tennessee game, Coach Dooley announced that Simon, who had led Georgia in rushing in 1979, would not make the trip to Tennessee because of an injury. It was also divulged that Walker would not start, although Dooley indicated that he, along with Young, would be one of four freshmen who could immediately provide help for the 1980 team. Two days later McMickens was proclaimed the starter, despite having rushed for only 121 yards on 31 carries in his career at Georgia and never having started a game.

On a sweltering, 90-degree night in Knoxville, Tennessee, in front of the largest crowd ever to see a game in the South (95,288), Georgia opened as three-point underdogs. The Volunteers' offensive coordinator was Bill Pace, who held the same position at Georgia the previous six seasons (1974 to 1979).

Fumbles, penalties, and poor punting plagued Georgia during the first half, as Tennessee built a 9–0 lead in the second quarter. As he watched teammate Norris break a 16-yard gain, Walker later said that he muttered to himself, "Oh, God, I may not be out there for a long time." However, as Georgia's offense became ineffective, Walker was inserted into the game midway through the second quarter. At the site of the enormous, orange-clad Neyland Stadium, Walker said that he was nearly "paralyzed. I didn't know what was going on." He gained two yards on his first collegiate rushing attempt. Dooley later said that he used "instinct" to send Walker into the game when he did.

The Volunteers passed for a touchdown in the third quarter and built their lead to 15–0. The Bulldogs were forced to punt again on the ensuing drive but caught a break for the first time all night. Georgia's Jim Broadway was only punting because starter Mark Malkiewicz had sustained an injury earlier in the week when teammate Freddie Gilbert blocked a punt of his in practice and injured the punter in the process. Broadway's punt was fumbled when Joe Happe, who had broken his hand in the second quarter, blindsided Tennessee returner Bill Bates. There was a mad scramble for Bates's bobble that continued until the ball rolled out of the Tennessee end zone for a Georgia safety.

Late in the third quarter, Georgia drove to Tennessee's 16-yard line. Quarterback Buck Belue turned and handed the football to the 218-pound Walker, who pounded through the Volunteers' defense, as described by the legendary Larry Munson:

> Tennessee leading 15–2, the crowd roaring against Georgia trying to make them drop it so they can't hear. We hand it off to Herschel, there's a hole, five, 10, 12, he's running over people!
>
> Oh, you Herschel Walker!
>
> My God almighty, he ran right through two men, Herschel ran right over two men, they had him dead away inside the 9.
>
> Herschel Walker went 16 yards, he drove right over orange shirts, just driving and running with those big thighs.
>
> My God, a freshman!

A star was born that night in Knoxville as Walker bowled over safety-man Bates and split two other defenders on his way to a 16-yard score. Early in the final quarter, Tennessee quarterback Jeff Olszewski fumbled, and Georgia recovered on the host's 25-yard line. With 11:16 remaining in the game, Walker scored again as he took a pitch to his left and danced around the end for a touchdown. Rex Robinson's extra point gave the Bulldogs a 16–15 lead.

Tennessee would later reach Georgia's 5-yard line, but linebacker Nate Taylor, the "Ty Ty Termite," forced a fumble recovered by Georgia's Pat McShea. Late in the game, Georgia was backed up against its own goal line when Walker took a pitch in his own end zone and ran the ball out just enough to give the Bulldogs some punting room. The backup Broadway boomed a 47-yard punt, and Georgia's defense held onto the one-point advantage for a victory.

After McMickens and Norris combined to rush for 39 yards on 12 carries, Walker, the third-string tailback, carried the ball 24 times for 84 yards. Although Walker's statistics were far from spectacular, he showcased tremendous power and maneuvers that he had not displayed in preseason practices. Certainly, there was no longer any doubt as to who was Georgia's starting tailback.

93-Yard Miracle

Split end Lindsay Scott's first two seasons as a Bulldog began unlike any other receiver's at Georgia. As a freshman and sophomore, Scott had caught a combined 70 passes for nearly 1,000 yards and gained more than 1,000 yards on kick returns. At least more of the same was expected from the talented Scott as a junior in 1980.

However, things went downhill for Scott during the spring before the season began. He first purposely pushed an academic counselor in his dorm room when the counselor attempted to break up a fight between Scott and his girlfriend. Scott lost his scholarship for an entire year over the incident. That summer, Scott lost control of his car, and landed in the hospital with a concussion and dislocated bones in his foot.

George Haffner from Texas A&M was Georgia's new offensive coordinator in 1980. It was believed the Bulldogs would be passing much more than previous seasons and Scott would be on the receiving end of many of the passes. Although he overcame his injuries and began the season healthy, his influence, and Georgia's passing game for that matter, was hardly evident by November 1980. The Bulldogs' offense revolved around Walker's running, and Scott played a marginal role compared to the previous two seasons. Through the first eight games of 1980, he ranked second on the team in receiving, having caught only 11 passes and no touchdowns. In addition, Scott was no longer Georgia's main kick returner, relinquishing those duties to the faster Walker and cornerback Scott Woerner.

According to author Loran Smith, Scott and roommate Buck Belue conversed the night before Georgia's game with Florida on November 8. At Jacksonville's Ramada Inn, Scott asked his quarterback, "Buck, you realize I haven't caught a touchdown pass since the Florida game last year?" He added, "I don't even remember what it's like to catch a touchdown pass."

The following afternoon, the Bulldogs entered their game against the Gators with a perfect 8–0 record. Second-ranked Georgia had its sights on an SEC title and perhaps even a national championship.

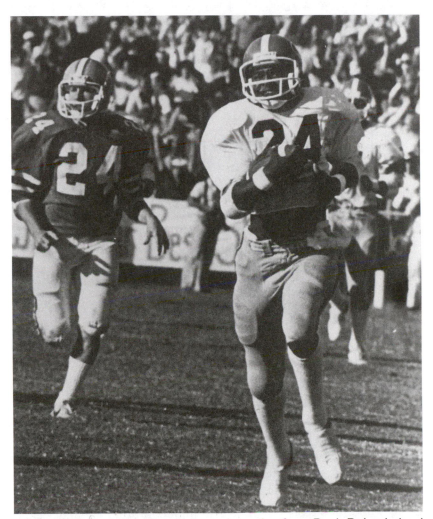

Lindsay Scott's 93-yard touchdown reception from Buck Belue helped the Bulldogs stun Florida and saved their 1980 national championship season. Photo courtesy of the University of Georgia.

Georgia led comfortably 20–10 at the start of the final quarter. Suddenly, Florida's passing attack, led by freshman quarterback Wayne Peace and receiver Tyrone Young, began exposing Georgia's defense. Peace and Young hooked up for a 54-yard gain that led to a Florida touchdown, and Peace passed to Young for a two-point conversion following the score. Young, who entered the contest without having caught a single pass all year, caught 10 passes against the Bulldogs for 183 yards. This still ranks as the third-most receiving yards by an individual against Georgia in a single game.

With 6:52 remaining in the game, a field goal by Florida's Brian Clark gave the Gators a 21–20 lead. Georgia was forced to punt, followed by a Florida punt, and fewer than two minutes remained in the game. It appeared the Bulldogs would soon experience their first loss of the season.

With the ball on its own 8-yard line, Georgia lost a yard on two plays and faced third down and 11 with 1:20 left in the game. "Realistically," said Coach Dooley afterward, "you had to figure that Florida had won the game." As some Georgia fans began to leave the Gator Bowl, a few Florida players to celebrate by dancing the funky chicken. And as the Gators' defense apparently relaxed, Left 76 was the play called by Haffner, hoping to gain a first down.

Belue rolled to his right, waved to Scott to cut to his left, and completed a pass to Scott near the 25-yard line. A Florida defense whose philosophy all season had been to bend but not break suddenly broke as Scott turned upfield and began to streak down the sideline. "I knew that Florida players were close behind me," Scott later said. "I could just feel it, but I was also determined that I was going to score."

Score he did. Scott raced into the end zone, completing a 93-yard miracle. Florida's James Jones, who was on the sidelines during "the Play," later said, "I was watching [Scott's run] and crying at the same time." One could imagine many other Gator players and fans were also shedding some tears.

Down 26–21, Florida had the football with approximately one minute remaining. Peace was subsequently intercepted by cornerback Mike Fisher, ending any chance of a second miracle. A thrilled Scott commented on his preseason troubles following Georgia's phenomenal win: "All that adversity is behind me now.... I just want to help this team stay undefeated." Scott did help Georgia stay undefeated and, in addition, helped propel the Bulldogs to number one in the polls.

On the same afternoon, Coach Bill Curry of Georgia Tech was carried off the field by his players following the Yellow Jackets' stunning tie of top-ranked Notre Dame. Georgia Tech, Georgia's bitter rival, had performed a gigantic favor for the Bulldogs. When the polls were released the following week, there would be a new number-one team in the country.

We're Number One!

By the 1980 season, the University of Georgia had been the recipient of nearly every accolade possible in its 86 seasons of football except winning a national championship. (Georgia's consensus national championship of 1942, where six polls recognized by the NCAA selected the Bulldogs number one, was not acknowledged until years later.) After finishing the 1980 regular season with an unscathed 11–0 record, Georgia finally had the opportunity to seize a national title as it met Notre Dame in the Sugar Bowl on January 1, 1981.

The Fighting Irish had the best all-around defense in the nation as it finished in the top eight in total defense, scoring defense, rushing defense, and passing defense. In addition, Georgia's Dooley had a 2–7 bowl record since 1967, while Coach Dan Devine of Notre Dame had won seven of nine bowl appearances. The Fighting Irish were a slight favorite to defeat the Bulldogs, but Notre Dame All-American Scott Zettek believed they should have been favored by as many as 10 points. A few days prior to the game, Zettek disrespectfully said that freshman sensation Walker only ran "well because his offensive line blocks well. Anyone could run through those holes," Zettek said. "They could pick somebody off the street."

Coach Dooley is carried off the field after Georgia defeated Notre Dame 17–10 in the Sugar Bowl on January 1, 1981, completing the Bulldogs' unbeaten, untied, national championship season.

The week of the Sugar Bowl, Georgia fans were absolutely wild and reportedly partied more than the annual New Orleans Mardi Gras crowd. A New Orleans bartender of many years said he thought Alabama fans had been the heaviest drinkers during their visits in 1978 and 1979, but he was going to award the national drinking championship to the Bulldogs followers.

A sold-out crowd of 77,895 packed the Superdome, including President Jimmy Carter and approximately 200 in his presidential party. Notre Dame, a run-oriented team, surprisingly came out throwing the ball and drove for the first score of the game—a 50-yard field goal by Harry Oliver only 4:19 into the contest. With 5:23 remaining in the opening quarter, the Fighting Irish lined up for another field goal, but Oliver's kick was blocked by seldom-used freshman Terry Hoage. Fewer than four minutes later, Georgia's Rex Robinson attempted to tie the score with a field goal. Robinson was one of the greatest place-kickers in college football history. His 56 career field goals and 101 consecutive extra points were both second-most in NCAA history. But the only other time Robinson had kicked in a dome (1978 Bluebonnet Bowl against Stanford), the normally accurate kicker missed two points after and two field goals. This time, however, Robinson's field goal of 46 yards was successful, and the Bulldogs had tied the game 3–3.

On the ensuing kickoff, Notre Dame's return men Jim Stone and Ty Barber inexplicably did not field the kick, likely because they thought the other would return the kick or that the ball would go into the end zone. Nevertheless, the football took a bounce inside Notre Dame's 5-yard line and was free. Bob Kelly of Georgia raced downfield and recovered the loose ball on the Fighting Irish's 1-yard line. Two plays later, Walker dove into the end zone for the game's first touchdown.

On Notre Dame's next drive, fullback John Sweeney fumbled and Chris Welton recovered for the Bulldogs on Notre Dame's 22-yard line. Three Walker carries later and it was another score for Georgia, which now led 17–3 with nearly three entire quarters left to play.

Although Notre Dame would score a touchdown late in the third quarter, mistakes and missed scoring opportunities tormented the Fighting Irish the entire game. Following Walker's second score, Notre Dame drove to Georgia's 13-yard line, where it faced fourth down and three. In his only pass attempt of the game, quarterback Mike Courey was intercepted by Scott Woerner in the end zone. With nine minutes remaining on the clock, quarterback Blair Kiel was intercepted by cornerback Mike Fisher. With three minutes left in the game and facing fourth down and one on Georgia's 48-yard line and down by seven points, Kiel was intercepted by Woerner on what would be Notre Dame's last possession.

Georgia ran out the remaining 2:56 left on the clock in 10 plays, including a seven-yard completion from Belue to Arnold on third down and seven with 2:05 remaining. This was Belue's only completion of the game in 12 attempts. With 14 seconds left in the game and Georgia not having to run another play, the Superdome's surface was flooded with red-attired Bulldogs fans who had stormed the field in celebration. Writer Lewis Grizzard heard a police officer on the floor of the dome say, "Thank God [the fans] ain't armed." A security guard screamed, "I've got the damn president of the United States in here, and I can't get him out!" A Notre Dame band member said, "If it meant that much, I'm glad Georgia won." It did mean that much. The University of Georgia had just captured its first national championship in any sport.

Walker was named the Sugar Bowl's Most Valuable Player with 90 votes and had the distinction of rushing for more yardage (150) than the total number of yards his entire team netted (127). Woerner, who intercepted two passes and gained 70 yards in total kick returns, was second in the MVP voting with 53½ votes.

Football is a sport where, like life itself, if many mistakes are made, it is difficult for one to succeed. Notre Dame gained 201 more yards than the Bulldogs (328–127), possessed the ball for nearly 10 more minutes (34:41–25:19), permitted Georgia's quarterback to complete only a single pass, and allowed the Bulldogs to convert just two of 16 third downs. However, the Fighting Irish missed two field goals, had another blocked, lost a fumble, misplayed a kickoff, and threw three interceptions.

After the victory, a triumphant Coach Dooley said of his Bulldogs, "This is the fightingest team I've ever coached…. People say we have good fortune, but I know this team makes many of its own breaks, and that's why we are here."

chapter 15

Georgia's Finest Class

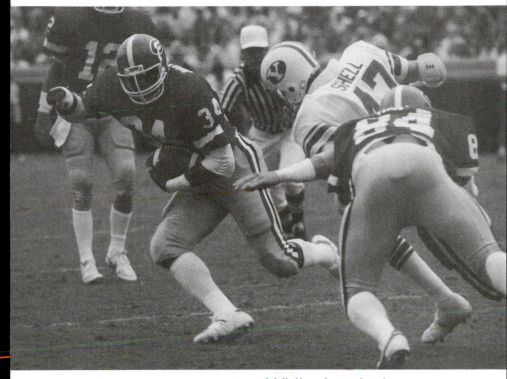

While the elusive Herschel Walker was able to grab the Heisman Trophy in his third season, the 1982 national championship just slipped out of Georgia's grasp.

Transformations Following the National Title

Following the 1980 national championship, Georgia football experienced several changes leading up to the next year. After 17 seasons, defensive coordinator Erk Russell departed Athens to develop a football program and serve as the head coach at Georgia Southern College. The other big change came when the east end of Sanford Stadium was closed and nearly 19,000 more seats were added to the stadium.

With the nearly $12 million addition to Sanford Stadium, its capacity grew from approximately 60,000 to 78,535 seats. With the additional seating, Georgia ranked fifth in the nation in home attendance in 1981, compared to 16th in 1980. This resulted in Georgia ranking among the NCAA's top 10 in home football attendance for only the second time since 1957.

For Georgia's first game of the '81 season, a home date with Tennessee at 1:30 PM, roughly 30,000 cars converged into Athens, or about 10,000 more than usual. With the expansion of the stadium came a reduction in parking permits, decreasing from 6,500 in 1980 to 3,500 but costing three times as much. It was reported that for the first game, cars had to be parked everywhere around the stadium and university, including sidewalks and grassy areas.

Despite the added complications, interest in Georgia football was at an all-time high. Perhaps no interest was greater than that of John "Kid" Terrell. Terrell was president of a bank in Comer, Georgia, and member of the Bulldog Club and the Bulldog Traveling Squad Inc. It appears that Terrell, a student at Georgia in the 1940s, enrolled in a beginning tennis course at the university to become the only individual who was a student at UGA during the days of Frank Sinkwich (lettered 1940–1942), Charley Trippi (1942, 1945–1946), and Herschel Walker (1980–1982).

With the expansion of the stadium came an end to the track fans who once sat on the railroad tracks outside of Sanford Stadium to view the games free of charge. For the Tennessee game, however, there were still about a dozen fans on the tracks, compared to as many as 2,000 track fans in previous years. The dozen or so dedicated fans could no longer see their Bulldogs from the tracks and faced an enormous side of concrete. Nevertheless, they did not seem to mind as long as there was whiskey to drink and Larry Munson on the radio calling the game.

In previous seasons, fans could also see the games from the bridge that ran along the stadium's west end. In 1981, however, the university placed a plywood barrier on the fence, obstructing view into the stadium. One Georgia fan and his friends desperately tried to find ways to see the Georgia-Tennessee game without a ticket. After being unsuccessful, the dejected fan said, "Looks like we ain't gonna get in.

"Heck," he said. "I gotta be at my wedding rehearsal at 4:00 anyway."

In 1981, Bill Lewis replaced the well-liked and much respected Russell as Georgia's defensive coordinator. One thing that had not changed from the year before was the Bulldogs' superior play. Against Tennessee, the defense was spectacular, shutting out the Volunteers while yielding only 152 total yards. Walker rushed for 161 yards and Buck Belue completed 10 of 15 passes for 140 yards and two touchdowns in a 44–0 Georgia victory.

On the day of the season opener, Uga III, Georgia's mascot since 1972, was retired during a pregame ceremony. He was dying of cancer but had been able to bear a pure-white off spring, and his heir apparent—seven-month-old Uga IV.

> Now the sun is sinking low,
> It's time for Uga III to go.
> Drifting toward a peaceful shore,
> To leave a place for Uga IV.
> —David Barrow

Dislike under the Lights

From the late 1970s to the mid-1980s, there was likely no other rival for Georgia more hated than the Clemson Tigers. The Bulldogs' only regular-season loss in 1981 had occurred at Clemson, while the

Tigers, like Georgia in 1980, would eventually finish the year with a 12–0 record and win the national championship.

Georgia played Clemson at night on Labor Day for its first game of 1982. Lights costing $800,000 and containing 432 bulbs were erected at Sanford Stadium to, among other reasons, accommodate television's 9:00 broadcast of the Georgia-Clemson contest. A night game had not been played at Sanford Stadium since 1951. The stadium's original lights were taken down with the arrival of athletic director Joel Eaves in 1964. Bill Hartman, who had played and coached at Georgia for decades, indicated that the Bulldogs began hosting only day affairs in the early 1950s because night games in Athens did not draw much of a crowd. For instance, in Georgia's last home night game in '51 against LSU, only an estimated 18,000 seats were filled.

The 1982 Georgia-Clemson game was not considered merely a football game, but a war between the national champions from the two previous seasons. The week of the game, Craig Hertwig, an All-American offensive lineman for Georgia in 1974, expressed his hatred for the Tigers: "Clemson ain't nothing but an imitation.... In the Atlantic Coast Conference [Clemson's conference], they play imitation football." Hertwig added, "I even hear they're going to put up imitation grass in the stadium up there [at Clemson] so the homecoming queen won't graze on it."

On the day of the game, there were numerous signs and banners bad-mouthing the opponent. One pro-Georgia sign read, "What do you call a No. 1 Clemson team? A cheetah." Earlier that spring, Clemson was placed on probation stemming from recruiting violations during the late 1970s. Another banner directed at Clemson, which confused a particular seven-year-old, read: "You might be Number One but you smell like Number Two." I distinctly remember asking my mother what the banner meant.

During summer practice, Walker had broken his right thumb. There was speculation for weeks leading up to the Clemson game whether or not Walker would play. Despite Vince Dooley's announcement that Walker would miss the season opener and Georgia would also be without three additional starters, the Bulldogs were a half-point favorite over the Tigers.

In front of 82,122 fans, Clemson scored first in the opening quarter on a six-yard run by quarterback Homer Jordan, a native Athenian. In the second quarter, Georgia tied the score following a blocked Tigers punt by Dale Carver that Stan Dooley recovered and then fell into the end zone for a Bulldogs touchdown. Also in the second quarter, Walker was inserted into the game for the first time as most of the sold-out crowd became hysterical. Georgia's Kevin Butler later kicked a field goal, and the Dogs led 10–7 at halftime.

Butler added his second field goal in the third quarter as the Bulldogs took a six-point lead. Clemson's Jordan was intercepted on the Tigers' final two possessions of the game, both occurring inside Georgia's 40-yard line. The first was corralled by roverback Terry Hoage, and the second was picked-off by linebacker Nate Taylor to seal the 13–7 win. Prior to his interception, Taylor told his fellow defenders in the huddle, "This is the last play in the world. Let's make it a good one."

Walker, nursing his injured thumb and used primarily as a decoy, finished with only 20 rushing yards on 11 carries. Fullback Barry Young led the Bulldogs in rushing with only 28 yards on three carries—Georgia had more passing yards than rushing (140–101) for the first time since the Clemson game the year before.

Jordan's homecoming was disastrous despite scoring Clemson's only touchdown of the game. Georgia's defense limited the senior quarterback to 135 total offensive yards in 37 plays and intercepted him four times.

The Georgia victory in the nighttime battle of number ones was its first of 11 consecutive wins. By the end of the 1982 regular season, the Bulldogs found themselves in the exact same situation as two years before: they were a perfect 11–0 and perched atop college football's rankings as the top team in the nation.

Herschel Wins Heisman

On December 4, 1982, as Georgia waited for its national title game with Penn State in the Sugar Bowl nearly a month later, tail-back Walker traveled to New York City for the presentation of the

Heisman Trophy. Walker signed autographs and posed for pictures in an Atlanta airport terminal and when he landed in New York, where he was met by a television crew. As he walked through the airport, a New Yorker with a distinct accent shouted, "How 'bout them Dogs!"

A television reporter asked Walker if it was one of the biggest days of his life. "I come from a little town called Wrightsville," he replied. "Things like this don't happen down there." Prior to the announcement of the 1982 Heisman winner, Sinkwich, Georgia's Heisman Trophy recipient 40 years earlier, revealed to the *Atlanta Constitution* that he had voted for Herschel. All previous winners of the trophy have the opportunity to vote every season. "I didn't think it was fair to try to pick the best player in all of college football until three years ago," said Sinkwich. "The first time I saw Herschel Walker play football, I knew you could pick one player."

Dressed in a red blazer, Walker received the 48th Heisman Trophy presented by the Downtown Athletic Club of New York. He was only the seventh junior and second native Georgian to receive the award. Quarterback John Elway of Stanford, the trophy's runner-up, must have a sensed Herschel would easily win—he didn't even show up for the ceremony. Walker won in a landslide.

A joyous Dooley said after the presentation, "I'm proud for Herschel, proud of our team, the coaches, for the University of Georgia and all the people Herschel touches." After receiving the award, Walker said, "This is the greatest thrill of my life for what the trophy stands for, not just an individual, but a team's performance for that season."

Dooley later said, "He's a tremendous talent as a football player and a tremendous human being."

After coming back to the University of Georgia to take final exams, Walker returned to the Downtown Athletic Club of New York for a banquet the Friday after receiving the award. "An award like this is not given to one person without him being around super people like I have been," said Walker. "It shows that dreams are possible and miracles can happen."

The speed and power exhibited by Walker were true miracles. And he was the key catalyst in making dreams become reality for

Bulldogs fans—33 Georgia victories and three SEC titles from 1980 to 1982.

New Bulldog Heroes

Walker announced in February 1983 that he was leaving Georgia early for the newly created professional league, the USFL. Although Walker's absence was certainly noteworthy, the Bulldogs did return several standout seniors for the 1983 season and were ranked 15th in the preseason Associated Press poll. By November, Georgia unexpectedly had achieved a 7–0–1 record and was ranked fourth entering its annual showdown with ninth-ranked Florida.

Georgia was seeking to keep its hopes alive for a fourth consecutive SEC championship, and Florida was looking to defeat the Bulldogs for the first time since 1977. Although Charley Pell had coached Florida to a respectable 29–14–1 record since 1980, he and his Gators had been unsuccessful in four tries against the Bulldogs. On the other hand, Coach Dooley had been extremely successful against Florida, achieving a 13–5–1 record, including having won eight of the last nine meetings. However, Coach Dooley and his Dogs would be facing what was probably Florida's best team since the late 1960s.

Florida ran a balanced offensive attack led by Wayne Peace, considered one of the best quarterbacks in the nation. Peace would be fortunate to be throwing against a Georgia pass defense minus All-American roverback Terry Hoage, who had sustained ankle and knee injuries. The Gators were favored by one point over the Bulldogs for the first time in six tries.

The 1983 Georgia-Florida game also signified a period when officials began to be more diligent in prohibiting spectators from bringing alcohol from the World's Largest Outdoor Cocktail Party inside the Gator Bowl. However, not all fans were deterred: "Diversion is the key [in bringing alcohol inside the stadium]," said a Georgia student. "You talk to the cop about his wife.... As long as you're not obvious."

A record 82,166 spectators filled the Gator Bowl to witness the 62nd meeting between Georgia and Florida. The Gators had first down and goal from Georgia's 1-yard line on their first series but had to settle for a field goal. Florida's Bobby Raymond would kick another field goal later in the first quarter and would add his third before halftime. Kevin Butler of Georgia kicked a second-quarter field goal, and the Bulldogs were fortunate to be trailing only 9–3 at the half. Florida squandered several scoring opportunities throughout the contest. In the second quarter, Peace was intercepted by Charlie Dean in Georgia's end zone.

With 5:44 remaining in the third quarter, Peace was intercepted by Daryll Jones, who stepped out of bounds on his own 1-yard line. At the time, Georgia had been outgained 318–97 in total yardage but only trailed by six points. Following the Jones interception, quarterback John Lastinger and the Bulldogs discovered their offense for the first time in the game and drove 99 yards in 16 plays. Fullback Barry Young scored from the 1-yard line with 13:18 left in the game, and Butler's extra point gave Georgia a 10–9 advantage.

Florida had an opportunity to retake the lead with 9:49 remaining in the game, but Raymond missed a 42-yard field goal. The missed kick was one of six occasions the Gators reached Georgia's 24-yard line or closer but came away without a touchdown.

Lastinger and roverback Gary Cantrell were Georgia's most outstanding players in the one-point victory. Lastinger, who had been undistinguished as the Bulldogs' starting quarterback for two seasons, was voted Georgia's Most Valuable Player, completing seven of 12 passes for 55 yards and rushing for 49 yards on 18 carries. Most significantly, he was instrumental in Georgia's game-winning 99-yard drive.

"It was just another in a series of adversities this team has had to overcome," said Dooley in regard to the victory. "Someone has always stepped forward and done the job. Tonight it was Gary Cantrell."

Junior Cantrell had suffered through injuries and had played very little in his three seasons at Georgia. Since Hoage was injured and backup rover John Little was lost to an injury on the third play of the game, Georgia's only option was to play Cantrell, a former scout team player. The third-string roverback responded by making eight tackles and breaking up a pass by Peace in a critical situation. The following week, the United Press International recognized Cantrell as the Southeast Defensive Player of the Week for his performance.

Defensive coordinator Bill Lewis had high praise for Cantrell: "A real success story. I bet he hasn't played 25 snaps in his career, and when he was called on in the biggest game of his life, he responded."

'Horns Caught Off Guard

Georgia lost to Auburn 13–7 in 1983, snapping the Bulldogs' 23 consecutive victories over SEC opponents four wins shy of the conference record. By finishing the season 9–1–1 and ranked seventh in both major polls, Georgia earned a trip to the Cotton Bowl to play Texas, the Southwest Conference champs and the second-ranked team in the nation.

The Longhorns were a perfect 11–0, with a defense regarded by some as the best ever in college football. Texas' defense ranked first in total defense, second in both passing defense and scoring defense, and fourth in rushing defense. It showcased first-team All-Americans linebacker Jeff Leiding and defensive backs Jerry Gray and Mossy Cade; 10 of the 11 starters would eventually be drafted by the NFL.

Earlier in the season, Texas had handed Auburn, the SEC champion, its only defeat of the season. Auburn, in turn, had dealt Georgia its only loss of 1983. The Longhorns were a heavy favorite over the Bulldogs by more than a touchdown. The probable victory over Georgia, coupled with a loss by top-ranked Nebraska to Miami later that night in the Orange Bowl, would propel Texas to first in the country.

Dressed in a new black fur coat, Walker, along with his wife, Cindy, was present at the Cotton Bowl to watch his old teammates. Two minutes before the scheduled kickoff time, both Georgia and Texas had yet to take the field. This prompted the public-address announcer to jest to the 67,891 fans: "We're looking for a great game if the two teams ever show up."

In an expected defensive battle, Georgia found itself behind 9–3 with fewer than five minutes remaining in the game. The Bulldogs faced fourth down and 17 in their own territory and decided to punt, hoping their defense could stop Texas one more time. The Longhorns, concerned about a possible fake punt, inserted safety Craig Curry as a return man. Georgia's Chip Andrews punted to Curry, who had never returned a punt in his collegiate career. "We were expecting a fake," said Curry after the game. As Andrews punted and while Curry awaited the football, Georgia's Gary Moss and Melvin Simmons pressured and surrounded the returner, with Simmons hollering, "Miss it, miss it!"

Curry heeded Simmons's request and dropped the punt. The ball then squirted from the grasp of teammate Jitter Fields, who had lined up behind Curry prior to the punt. Georgia's Moss recovered the fumble on Texas' 23-yard line with 4:32 left in the contest. The Bulldogs ran two times for six yards and faced third down and 4 on the 17-yard line. Quarterback Lastinger ran an option to his right. As he decided to run instead of pitch the ball, Curry chose to take Georgia's trailing tailback, Tron Jackson. As Curry bit on the play, Lastinger turned upfield and raced into the end zone for a 17-yard score. Kevin Butler's point after gave Georgia a 10–9 lead with 3:22 remaining in the game.

On its last possession, Texas could not gain a single first down, and the Bulldogs held on to the upset with a one-point victory. Although Georgia's offense only generated 215 total yards and Lastinger completed just six of 19 passes for 66 yards, threw an interception, and rushed for only 19 yards on 12 carries, the senior quarterback was selected Most Valuable Player of the bowl game.

Texas had seven offensive drives that reached Georgia's 33-yard line or closer but could only muster three field goals. Longhorn kicker Jeff Ward, who had made 14 consecutive field goals entering the game and appeared to be the game's MVP before Lastinger's scoring run, missed two field goals, and Texas committed four turnovers. Most significantly, Texas' anticipation of a fake punt that never occurred ultimately led to the Bulldogs' memorable win.

Lastinger, who had lost his starting quarterback job earlier in the 1983 season, was regarded as a below-average passer and runner during his time at Georgia. However, he was one of a large group of 1983 seniors who, in establishing an identity without Walker, just simply won ballgames. The win over Texas, according to Coach Dooley, was "a tribute to our senior class, one I think has to be the best in modern football. What they've accomplished in the last four years is really something."

What they accomplished was college football's best record from 1980 to 1983, 43–4–1, and by so doing they became the finest football senior class ever at the University of Georgia.

chapter 16

The Final Years of Dooley's Dogs

After a dominant run in the early 1980s, Vince Dooley had to do more of a balancing act in coaching overachieving teams for the remainder of the decade.

A Dream Come True

In 1984 Georgia was unranked in the Associated Press preseason poll for the first time in six seasons. In their opening game against Southern Miss, the Bulldogs underachieved and were fortunate to win by seven points. Next Georgia hosted Clemson, the number two–ranked team in the nation which had also received 15 of 52 first-place votes from Associated Press voters. The Tigers had won their first two games, albeit against Appalachian State and Virginia, by a combined score of 95–7 and were generally considered better than their national title team of 1981. They had also won 10 consecutive games, dating back to September 1983, by an average of nearly three touchdowns per win.

Clemson's dominant defensive line featured the Perrys, senior and 320-pound William "Refrigerator" and his lighter, younger brother, freshman Michael Dean. In addition, the Tigers' quarterback, senior Mike Eppley, had a 16–1–1 record as a starter and was the highest-rated passer in college football. The Georgia-Clemson game had an even 3–3–1 series record since 1977, with an average margin of defeat of fewer than six points. But the Tigers had a history of performing poorly in Athens—they had won only one of 21 games against the Bulldogs in the Classic City since 1915.

The week of the Clemson contest, Georgia kicker and All-American Kevin Butler interestingly had a reoccurring dream that the game was decided on his long field goal. In fact, the dream was so realistic to Butler that he devoted extra practice time to kicking field goals of 62 yards. In practice three days before the game, Butler was perfect on four attempts from that unlikely long distance.

Clemson had been playing like the second-ranked team in the country, and it led Georgia 20–6 at halftime. While Eppley had thrown for two first-half scores, the Bulldogs' quarterback, Todd Williams, threw four intercepted passes.

Following a fumble recovery by Georgia's Carlyle Hewatt early in the second half, Williams passed for a 19-yard touchdown to

Herman Archie. Late in the third quarter, the Bulldogs drove 66 yards to a one-yard scoring run by Cleveland Gary, and Georgia had tied the game at 20–20.

After another fumble recovery, this time by Calvin Ruff, the Dogs took their first lead on a 43-yard field goal by Butler with 6:03 remaining in the game. But the Tigers tied the game four minutes later on Donald Igwebuike's third field goal.

On Georgia's next and final drive, a 24-yard draw play by Tron "the Electron" Jackson helped place the Bulldogs in field position to attempt an extremely long field goal. With only 11 seconds remaining, Butler successfully and miraculously kicked a 60-yarder with at least five yards to spare. The lengthy field goal not only broke Butler's previous school mark of 59 yards but tied an SEC record.

On the ensuing kickoff, the Tigers returned the ball to Georgia's 35-yard line, but no time remained on the clock. Controversy developed when Clemson coach Danny Ford protested that not only did Georgia commit a personal foul against the Tigers' return man, but one second remained on the clock when he was bumped out of bounds. Ford's complaints to the referees were to no avail, and Georgia upset Clemson 26–23.

After a subpar first half, Georgia's Williams passed much more effectively in the final two quarters. The Bulldogs' running game was led by freshmen Gary (61 yards) and Lars Tate (48 yards). In addition, Jackson gained 47 yards. Although Georgia's defense yielded 356 total yards, it forced seven Clemson turnovers, all committed by quarterback Eppley. Georgia's Tony Flack was a standout on defense, responsible for two of Eppley's three interceptions.

Kevin Butler's dream of kicking a long field goal that would decide the Georgia-Clemson game became a reality. "I'm just glad I had a chance to win it for these guys," said Butler. "I've never seen a team fight back the way this one did." Still trembling as he was being interviewed, among Butler's postgame comments was an indication that he knew his 60-yard kick was good immediately after it left his foot.

And Then There Were Four

After being ranked eighth in the nation with a 7–1 record in early November, the Bulldogs ended the '84 season in disappointing fashion. Georgia dropped its final three games of the regular season to Florida, Auburn, and Georgia Tech, and then tied Florida State in the Citrus Bowl.

Georgia prepared for the 1985 season opener against Alabama, but defensive starters Steve Boswell and Jake Richardson would sit out for that game with injuries and center and All-American candidate Keith Johnson would miss the entire year because of back surgery. There was also a question as to who would start at quarterback. Georgia's top two passers from the prior season—Todd Williams and David Dukes—were injured, and James Jackson, chosen MVP of the '84 Citrus Bowl, had an aggravated ankle.

For the second time in four years, Georgia's first game would be played on Labor Day night in Athens against a prominent opponent. Unranked in the preseason AP poll for the second consecutive season, the Bulldogs were facing one of the better defenses in the nation, led by All-American linebacker Cornelius Bennett. Almost as anticipated as the game itself was the halftime ceremony during which Walker's No. 34 jersey would be retired.

It is far from commonplace for the University of Georgia to retire football jerseys, considering that only four have been retired in 115 years of football through the 2006 season. In 1985, Walker joined only Frank Sinkwich, Charley Trippi, and Theron Sapp to be accorded such an honor.

The night before the Alabama game, Coach Vince Dooley gave Walker, a well-known Snickers candy bar enthusiast, a yard's length of Snickers bars. "I figured for all the yards he's gained I'd give him a yard-long Snickers," said Dooley.

At halftime, with the score 7–3 in Alabama's favor, Walker stood beside the other three Georgia football immortals as his jersey was retired. Walker's jersey used in the ceremony was from his freshman year. It had been given to Sonny Seiler, owner of

mascot Uga. Seiler had kept the jersey until its retirement ceremony. The jersey would later be displayed at the Butts-Mehre
Heritage Hall athletic facility, which was in the process of being
constructed.

The Crimson Tide extended its lead to 13–3 in the fourth
quarter. In one of the most thrilling Georgia football games in
defeat, quarterback Wayne Johnson passed to Jimmy Hockaday
for an 11-yard touchdown with 4:21 left in the game. Johnson had
started the game, later was benched for James Jackson, but had
returned to rally the Bulldogs.

Alabama was forced to punt with under a minute remaining
from its 33-yard line. Georgia's Terrie Webster blocked Chris
Mohr's kick, which Calvin Ruff recovered in the end zone for a
Bulldogs touchdown. With only 50 seconds left on the clock and
losing 16–13, Alabama quarterback Mike Shula drove the
Crimson Tide down the field by completing four of five passes for
71 yards, climaxed by a 17-yard touchdown to Al Bell with only
seconds remaining. Alabama had stolen a 20–16 victory from the
Bulldogs. This would be the final of only five losses Coach Dooley
endured in 25 season-opening games.

By mid-November, it would be the only defeat experienced by
the Bulldogs in achieving a 7–1–1 record and a number-12
ranking, including a 24–3 victory over number-one Florida,
Georgia's only win in its history over a top-ranked team.

Back to Their Bread and Butter

As was the case for the previous two decades under Dooley,
Georgia had a highly productive running game during the mid-
1980s. In contrast, the Bulldogs' passing attack in 1984 and
1985 was ineffective, ranked last in the SEC both years and probably cost the team at least a couple of victories during the two
campaigns. As spring practice of 1986 began, Georgia was plan-
ning to throw the football more than previous seasons, despite the
presence of future NFL backs Tim Worley, Keith Henderson, and

Lars Tate, as well as fullback David McCluskey, the 13th all-time leading rusher at Georgia when he graduated.

Dooley declared that Georgia's offense in 1986 would not necessarily throw the ball with great frequency, but it would pass more effectively. He promised that it would be more exciting than previous seasons and that his Bulldogs would line up in a shotgun formation on their first offensive play of the year against Duke.

Dooley stayed true to his word as quarterback Jackson completed a nine-yard pass to Worley from the shotgun formation on the initial play of the season. The Bulldogs eventually trounced Duke 31–7, and their wide-open offense was never forced to punt. Georgia gained 269 rushing yards and 202 through the air, the most passing yards in a single game in nearly three years (216 against Clemson in 1983). The Dogs' defense was equally impressive and featured two sacks by sophomore Richard Tardits. Tardits was a defensive lineman from France who barely knew the rules of American football when he walked on at Georgia in 1985.

Jackson successfully guided the offense by completing 16 of 22 passes for 193 yards and a touchdown to tight end Troy Sadowski. In addition, he rushed for 54 yards on nine carries.

Following the win, Dooley approved of the balanced offensive attack displayed by his squad. "That is what I like, even though it is hard for me to convince people," said Dooley. "I like this. I want to do this, but I want to have confidence that we can do this."

For the most part, Georgia continued its passing tendencies throughout the season but with mixed results. The Bulldogs had a record of only 6–3, including upset losses to Clemson and Florida, as they faced number-eight Auburn at Jordan-Hare Stadium in a nighttime affair. If defeating the Tigers was not already difficult enough, Jackson did not join the team at Auburn as was expected. He was granted permission to attend his grandmother's funeral but, by mid-afternoon on Saturday, had not reported back to the team. Only a few hours prior to kickoff, Wayne Johnson, Georgia's backup quarterback, was told he would start against the Tigers.

Auburn had one of the nation's best defenses and a potent offense that starred quarterback Jeff Burger and tailback Brent Fullwood, a consensus All-American who would eventually finish sixth in the Heisman Trophy voting. The Tigers had the inside track on winning an SEC title and were 10½-point favorites over the Bulldogs—and that was prior to Jackson's absence.

Although Auburn assumed an early 7–0 lead, Georgia shockingly led 20–10 late in the game. Without Jackson under center, the Bulldogs productively did what they had done best for more than 20 seasons—run the ball. Georgia finished the game with 239 rushing yards, including 94 from Tate, Henderson's 62, and 45 from McCluskey. Wayne Johnson was responsible for both of the Bulldogs' touchdowns, throwing for an eight-yard score to Sadowski and later rushing for another. Although Johnson did not pass the ball often, he was extremely effective when he did. After throwing an incompletion on his first attempt, the sophomore signal-caller completed his last six passes for 59 yards.

Auburn drove 99 yards, ending with a Burger pass to Lawyer Tillman with 2:51 left in the game. Down 20–16, the Tigers forced Georgia to punt and got the ball back on their own 6-yard line with 1:43 remaining. Burger promptly began moving the offense toward a game-winning score. However, with 54 seconds left on the clock, he was intercepted a third time on Georgia's 33-yard line by linebacker Steve Boswell, securing the unexpected win.

The Bulldogs' defense, which held Fullwood to 16 rushing yards in the second half and 94 overall, was given credit for the victory, along with Georgia's fine running game. "Georgia's offensive front manhandled our defensive front," said Auburn coach and Georgia alum Pat Dye. "They just lined up and whipped us."

The 20–16 win over Auburn in 1986 may be best remembered for what happened following the game. Hundreds of Bulldogs fans rushed the field in celebration and began pulling up pieces of the turf for souvenirs. Ecstatic with the thrill of victory, Georgia fans also attempted to take down a goalpost. When this began to occur, security personnel began spraying the enthusiasts with water cannons, including innocent Georgia bystanders in the northeast corner of the stadium. It was the first time Jordan-Hare Stadium used its water cannons for crowd control, Georgia won for the first time in 11 years against a double-digit favorite.

Number 200

For the second consecutive season in 1988, a loss to Auburn denied Georgia a trip to the Sugar Bowl and the 11th SEC title in school history. In 1988, the 20–10 defeat by the Tigers also resulted in Dooley's 200th career victory being placed on hold. With the regular-season finale against Georgia Tech and a meeting with Michigan State in the Gator Bowl remaining on the schedule, Dooley and his Dogs hoped to improve the coach's unequalled 199–77–10 record at Georgia. A few days prior to the Georgia Tech game, All-SEC center Todd Wheeler declared, "I'd like to be on the team that gave him his 200th. And I don't want to wait until the Gator Bowl to do it."

The Bulldogs in '88 had an explosive running game and quarterbacks—Wayne Johnson and Greg Talley—who were efficient passers. Tailbacks Tim Worley and Rodney Hampton and fullback Keith Henderson led a rushing offense that ranked first in the SEC. Georgia's weakness, however, was its passing defense, which ranked last in the conference. The Dogs had allowed four of their opponents to pass for more than 320 yards in a single game and seemed especially vulnerable to teams that had balanced offenses.

Georgia Tech happened to have a balanced offensive attack and, in addition, the 13th-best defense in the nation, despite its 3–7 record. One of its few wins was a 34–0 thrashing of South Carolina, which had been ranked eighth in the country at the time and undefeated, including a 23–10 victory over Georgia.

Behind a John Kasay field goal and a Worley touchdown run, the Bulldogs held a 10–3 lead over the Yellow Jackets at halftime. In the third quarter, defensive tackle Wycliff Lovelace intercepted a Georgia Tech pass and returned it 33 yards for a score.

Lovelace, a fifth-year senior, had been a highly touted high school player. But because of three knee injuries and multiple position changes, he never was a standout player or a season's starter at Georgia until 1988. His interception return for a touchdown was a fitting ending to an erratic collegiate career in his last game at Sanford Stadium.

In the final quarter, Johnson threw a five-yard touchdown to Henderson, and Georgia eventually won 24–3. For the first time in more than six years the Bulldogs passed for more yards than they rushed for in a winning effort. Johnson completed 14 of 24 passes for 168 yards and was not intercepted. Worley, a dark-horse Heisman Trophy contender, was held to 43 rushing yards on 13 carries, but Hampton picked up the slack with 63 yards on just 10 attempts.

Nevertheless, Georgia mostly won the game because of what it had lacked all season—an unfaltering defense. The Yellow Jackets' offense could only muster 288 total yards, did not cross the Bulldogs' goal line, and committed four turnovers while forcing none from Georgia. In victory, the Bulldogs finished the season undefeated at home for the first time since 1982. Dooley's record against his intrastate rival improved to 19–6.

Most noteworthy, Vince Dooley had captured his 200th victory as the Bulldogs' head coach. In the final seconds of the game he asked his players not to give him a victory ride. He explained after the game that as he became older, he felt more compassion for the losing team and coach or, as he admitted later, "Maybe I'm afraid I'd heal slower if they dropped me."

As his wife, Barbara—who had never been on the field after a game—and other family members joined Dooley, the coach reminisced about his first victory at Georgia 24 years earlier against Vanderbilt in 1964. "At that time, I sure didn't think I'd still be around coaching today," he said.

Dooley ended his coaching career with a win in the Gator Bowl on January 1, 1989. In a quarter century of coaching, Dooley won 201 games, six SEC championships, a national championship in 1980, and was one of only 10 coaches in Division I-A history to win at least 200 games. Before Dooley's arrival, Georgia had just five winning campaigns in the previous 15 seasons (1949 to 1963) and only a 3–27–2 record against ranked opposition from 1947 through 1963. Coach Dooley, hired at only 31 years of age in December 1963 had only one losing season in 25 campaigns and compiled an impressive 33–33–4 record versus Associated Press–ranked opponents.

After his 200th victory, Dooley, as he had consistently done at Georgia, gave credit to everyone except himself. "Still, this is not a victory for me, but a victory for all the people who have been involved with the program over the years," said Dooley. "I've had the good fortune to be associated with a lot of great people."

It is apparent that the University of Georgia had the good fortune to have Dooley coach and guide its football program for a memorable 25-season tenure.

chapter 17
"Boy, It's Tough to Follow a Legend…"

Ray Goff found out soon enough that it's hard to follow a coaching legend when he succeeded Vince Dooley. Photo courtesy of Getty Images.

Lucky Dogs

Ray Goff became Georgia's 23rd head coach when he succeeded Vince Dooley in 1989. Goff had been a standout quarterback at Georgia from 1974 to 1976. He served as the Bulldogs' running back and tight end coach in addition to recruiting coordinator during the 1981 through 1988 seasons. In replacing Dooley, Goff had not only assumed the responsibility of guiding one of the most recognized football programs in the country but also the undaunted challenge of following a living coaching legend.

After a 2–0 start in Goff's first season, Georgia lost six of its final 10 games, including a one-point defeat by Syracuse in the Peach Bowl. In 1990, the Dogs' problems continued—six of their top nine defensive linemen from the spring of 1989 were either lost to injuries, quit the team, or became academically ineligible. In addition, Arthur Marshall, one of the premier receivers in the SEC, was lost for the season with a broken leg.

Georgia began the 1990 campaign with an 18–13 defeat by LSU. After only 13 games as the Bulldogs' head coach, Goff's job security was already a frequent topic of conversation among the Georgia faithful.

One week later, Georgia hosted Southern Miss and its stand-out quarterback Brett Favre as the Dogs attempted to avoid their first five-game losing streak since 1961. Favre had been in a car accident in July, undergone emergency surgery a month later, and told he may never play football again. Although he missed the Eagles' first game, he returned a week later to guide Southern Miss to an upset victory over number-13 Alabama.

Midway through the third quarter, Favre avoided a Georgia sack and launched a 62-yard scoring pass to Michael Jackson. Favre's second touchdown toss had given Southern Miss a 17–6 lead over Georgia. At this point in the game, many of the fans resorted to booing the Georgia team. The Bulldogs promptly responded, however, as Larry Ware rushed for a 20-yard touchdown on third down and six with 5:10 remaining in the quarter. With 6:04 left in the game, Ware would score again on a five-yard dash. However, for the second consecutive time, the Bulldogs did not convert on a two-point conversion and led Southern Miss by only a single point.

Georgia would get the ball back but was forced to punt from deep in its own territory. After a good punt return, the Eagles had the ball on Georgia's 24-yard line with 1:40 remaining in the game. After a yard lost on a rushing attempt and two incompletions by Favre, Southern Miss faced fourth down and 11 on the Bulldogs' 25-yard line. Kicker Jim Taylor, who had defeated Alabama the previous week on a 52-yard field goal, entered the game to attempt a game-winning 42-yarder with less than a minute remaining.

Taylor's kick appeared to be dead center after it was booted and looked good as it headed toward the goalpost. But at the last moment it tailed and bounced off the inside of the right upright and was no good. The same fans who were booing the Bulldogs only a quarter earlier were now in a frenzy. Georgia had defeated Southern Miss 18–17 on what was viewed as a gift from God.

Led by Ware's 77 rushing yards on 18 carries and freshman Garrison Hearst's 13 rushes for 72 yards, Georgia outrushed its opponent for the first time in seven games. Favre passed for 136 yards, two scores, and no interceptions, but his offense could only net 16 yards in the final quarter. The Eagles had defeated Alabama the week before and Florida State in 1989 and would later upset number-15 Auburn in November, but they could not beat the Bulldogs on a last-minute, ricocheted kick.

"We had an opportunity for our team to fold the tent," said Goff after the victory. "It was a chance to shut it down if you wanted to. But to our players' credit, they didn't."

After a 4–3 start to the '90 season, including a comeback victory over Alabama and barely beating East Carolina, Georgia suffered defeats in its last four games by an average of more than 18 points per game. Georgia's young and inexperienced team was manhandled in its final game by a Georgia Tech squad on its way to a national championship. During the game, a plane carrying a banner reading "Fire Ray Goof!" flew over Sanford Stadium.

Goff's two-year record at Georgia had been a disappointing 10–13. If his job security had been an issue before, it was really a concern now. It was becoming increasingly apparent to many that the Georgia football program needed a complete turnaround.

Frosh Zeier Zaps Tigers

Looking to reverse the substandard 1989 and 1990 seasons, Georgia's 1991 campaign was given the label of "Operation Turnaround." The coaching staff also experienced a major change in personnel, including the addition of Wayne McDuffie, formerly Georgia's offensive line coach from 1977 to 1981, who was appointed as the offensive coordinator. McDuffie would install a pro-style offense and take advantage of the skills of Eric Zeier, a highly touted freshman.

Although Zeier did not start the first four games of the year, he and the entire Georgia offense performed somewhat better than expected in compiling a 3–1 record. Next on the schedule was a home date with sixth-ranked Clemson. The Tigers sported the best defense in the nation (156.7 yards allowed per game) and had defeated the Bulldogs the year before 34–3. The game was only the fourth night game in Athens since new lights were installed at Sanford Stadium in 1982.

Clemson's Brenston Buckner, a sophomore defensive lineman from Columbus, Georgia, and an eventual two-time All-ACC selection, seemingly still bitter because Georgia did not recruit him out of high school, was quoted as saying, "I don't see anything special about playing between a bunch of trees [Sanford Stadium's hedges]. Growing up, that's all you used to hear, 'Vince Dooley between the hedges.' Man, it just got old."

Playing between the "trees" in front of a sellout crowd of 85,434, Georgia and Clemson were deadlocked at 3–3 late in the first quarter. Clemson's Rodney Williams took a handoff and began streaking downfield for an apparent touchdown. Suddenly, defensive back Mike Jones caught Williams from behind and stripped the ball out of his arms. Georgia's George Wynn recovered the fumble on the Bulldogs' 27-yard line. Clemson had committed a critical and game-changing turnover.

Things took a positive step for Goff and the Bulldogs when freshman quarterback Eric Zeier began to come into his own. At times it seemed the Georgia program was headed back to prominence.

Late in the first half, excitement ensued at Sanford Stadium when a double bank of lights unexpectedly went out on the stadium's south side. After a brief delay, the game resumed in the partially lit stadium. All lighting was not fully restored until just before the start of the second half.

With less than a minute before halftime, Zeier, who had not started but relieved Greg Talley after just two possessions, and the Bulldogs had the ball on their own 43-yard line. The freshman phenom passed long to Arthur Marshall for a 49-yard gain and, on the next play, connected with Andre Hastings for an eight-yard touchdown with only 13 seconds until the half.

In the third quarter, Georgia's Kanon Parkman and Clemson's Nelson Welch traded field goals, and the Bulldogs led 13–6 heading into the fourth quarter. Early in the final quarter, Zeier passed to Hastings for another touchdown, but Clemson crossed Georgia's goal line for the first time with 4:29 remaining in the game. A couple of minutes later, behind only 20–12, the Tigers turned the ball over on downs on their own 15-yard line. Three plays later, Garrison Hearst rushed for a one-yard score, and the Dogs prevailed 27–12.

Georgia gained 360 yards against college football's best defense. Although Clemson shut down the Bulldogs' run, they could not stop "Air Georgia"—Zeier passed for 249 yards, two touchdowns, and no interceptions. Marshall had six receptions for 128 yards, while Hastings caught five passes and both of Zeier's touchdown tosses.

In what would be Clemson's only loss during the regular season, Georgia had finally won a game it was not supposed to win. To date, the victory over the Tigers, an eight-point favorite, is the biggest upset victory for Georgia at Sanford Stadium since 1973. The 15-point win over the Tigers was due in large part to Zeier. "Eric did a good job," said McDuffie following the game. "That freshman quarterback won't throw it up for grabs. He knows what he's doing."

There is no doubt turnovers also played a key role in Georgia's victory. Georgia committed only one turnover while forcing five from Clemson, including the game's key play—Williams's fumble after being stripped by Jones. "You have to give Georgia credit," said Williams. "They just came out and kicked our butts."

Time Runs Out on Auburn

As Georgia was preparing for its next-to-last regular-season game of 1992 against Auburn, the focus was not necessarily on what had happened during the Bulldogs' successful season but what could have been. After winning nine games the previous year, Georgia had lofty expectations for the '92 campaign. Prior to the Auburn game, the Bulldogs were 7–2, ranked 12th in the nation, and had an excellent chance of achieving their most successful season in nine years. However, many believed that Georgia should have been 9–0 with the possibility of playing for a national championship instead.

Featuring quarterback Zeier, scatback Hearst, receiver Hastings, and offensive tackle Alec Millen, Georgia's offense was the seventh best in the nation and given the majority of the credit for the Bulldogs' accomplishments. Georgia's defense, however, despite only yielding slightly more than 300 yards a game and having college football's sixth-best scoring defense, was primarily held accountable for close losses to Tennessee and Florida.

Against the Volunteers, Georgia had a 31–27 late lead until allowing Tennessee to convert a fourth-down-and-14 pass for a first down from its 30-yard line. The Vols eventually drove down the field to score and win 34–31. Seven weeks later, the Bulldogs trailed Florida 23–7 in the second quarter only to come back and pull within two points. Late in the game, the Gators faced third down and 13 in their own territory. If Georgia had stopped Florida and forced a punt, the resurging Bulldogs would have only needed a field goal for victory. Instead, while communication problems occurred between Georgia's defensive unit and coaches on the sideline, Florida's Shane Matthews scrambled out of the pocket to complete a 14-yard pass for a first down. The Gators ran out the clock and defeated the Bulldogs 26–24.

Interestingly in the Florida game, Matthews claimed he was bitten by a Georgia defensive player early in the contest. He stated the bite occurred in a pileup following a play, so he had no idea which player was responsible. Astonished and baffled about Matthew's allegations, no player owned up to the biting. "It is hard to bite somebody through a mouthpiece and a face mask," pointed out linebacker Charlie Clemons.

Auburn had its own troubles during the 1992 season. News had been released recently that the school was being investigated by the NCAA for nine rules violations, including one involving head coach Pat Dye. Taped conversations from a few years earlier had been uncovered where Dye and an Auburn booster apparently spoke with a player about illegal benefits. In addition to "Tigergate," despite having the fourth-best defense in the nation, allowing only 249.9 total yards per game, the Tigers were experiencing a disappointing 5–3–1 season.

In a defensive battle, Georgia and Auburn fought to a 7–7 tie in the first half, where each team penetrated the other's side of the field on just one occasion. Early in the second half, Zeier completed a 64-yard pass to Hearst for a touchdown. It was one of Hearst's two touchdowns in the game, in addition to 105 rushing yards on 31 carries, adding to his candidacy for the Heisman Trophy. Leading 14–10 with 3:52 left in the game, Georgia seemed to clinch the win when Al Jackson intercepted a Stan White pass in the end zone. However, Georgia was soon forced to punt. With 2:36 remaining in the contest, White moved Auburn 40 yards to Georgia's 5-yard line, where the Tigers called their final timeout. On the next play, Orlando Parker nearly scored on a run, but he was driven out of bounds inside Georgia's 1-yard line with 19 seconds left on the clock.

From only about one foot from Georgia's goal line, White took the snap from his center and moved to his left. As he attempted to hand the ball to tailback James Bostic, it bounced into the air off of fullback Joe Frazier's arm and shoulder pad. A mad scramble ensued for the ball that was finally recovered by Bostic. While both teams argued about who had possession and where to spot the ball, Georgia coach Goff was frantically motioning and screaming for his players to stay down. Linebacker Mitch Davis admitted later that he purposely laid on an Auburn player so the Tigers could not line up and run another play. During all of the confusion, the clock at Jordan-Hare Stadium ran out. Georgia won.

While the referees immediately left the playing field, Georgia players, coaches, and fans celebrated and Auburn's were bewildered and irate. Auburn defensive coordinator Wayne Hall supposedly attempted to confront the officials as to why they had not spotted the football sooner so the Tigers could run an additional play. In the process, Hall began to hyperventilate so badly it was believed he was having a heart attack. As Hall was being escorted out of the stadium in a police patrol car, Georgia assistant coach Frank Orgel had to defend himself in the players' tunnel against an attacking Auburn fan.

After the game, Auburn players and coaches bitterly complained that they should have been able to run another play because the referee had been slow in spotting the football. Comments made by the Tigers included, "The better team didn't win today," and, "We won."

However, it was the Bulldogs who actually won 14–10, thanks to a fantastic performance by their defense. "I can't actually say enough good things about our defense," said Goff after the victory. "The defense has been maligned and talked about." The defense continued to be talked about throughout the rest of the season, but in a positive manner. With two admirable performances against Georgia Tech and Ohio State in the Citrus Bowl, Georgia finished the season 10–2 and ranked eighth in both major polls— its best record and highest ranking since 1983.

Goff's Crippled Canines

Georgia followed its success in 1992 with depressing seasons in '93 and '94. Even with Zeier at quarterback, the Bulldogs only had an 11–10–1 combined record and made no bowl appearances because of poor defensive play. Athletics director Dooley gave head coach Goff an ultimatum prior to the 1995 season: achieve "significant improvement" in the present campaign or not be around to coach in 1996.

The season started off in spectacular fashion with a 42–23 victory over South Carolina, where Georgia outscored the Gamecocks 35–9 in the second half. Quarterback Mike Bobo threw for 250 yards and two touchdowns, receiver Hines Ward had 103 receiving yards, while the Bulldogs' defense limited South Carolina to 29 rushing yards. The highlight of the win was the performance by scatback Robert Edwards, who had played cornerback the previous two seasons. The ex-defender rushed for 169 yards and tied a school record by scoring five touchdowns.

Georgia led heavily favored Tennessee 24–20 late in the third quarter the following week but was eventually defeated 30–27. Despite the loss to the Volunteers, the Bulldogs actually appeared in both major polls at number 23. Edwards rushed for 156 yards and averaged more than 10 yards per carry but suffered a season-ending fractured foot.

Edwards's fractured foot would be the beginning of a rash of injuries sustained by Georgia throughout the season. Standout Bobo was lost for the season two weeks later with a fractured knee. A month later, backup quarterback Brian Smith separated a shoulder. By the end of the season, Georgia's starting quarter-back, sophomore Ward, who had not played the position since high school, was playing with a broken bone in his wrist. Because of additional injuries, the Bulldogs had seven running backs miss at least one game with an injury, while six different scatbacks started the first eight games of the season. The low point of Georgia's injury epidemic was when Odell Collins, another running back, pulled a hamstring in late October while doing his laundry and missed the rest of the year.

Following a 37–31 loss to Auburn, Georgia's record dropped to 5–5 and Goff, who had not coached the Bulldogs to "significant improvement," was forced to resign. Goff's apparent final game was a Thanksgiving Day meeting with favored Georgia Tech, which, like Georgia, had aspirations for a bowl bid.

Hines Ward, who would go onto NFL stardom and win the MVP award of Super Bowl XL, was one of the great players to come out of the Georgia program in the 1990s.

Seemingly, the Yellow Jackets' bowl game aspirations were to be fulfilled as quarterback Donnie Davis threw two second-quarter touchdown passes to give Georgia Tech the lead 14–0. In the third quarter, Georgia's Torin Kirtsey rushed for a 10-yard score to cut the Bulldogs' deficit in half. Early in the final quarter, Georgia Tech kicked a field goal and comfortably led 17–7. However, Ward led the Dogs down the field to a six-yard touchdown run by Kirtsey with 8:51 left in the game. Ward's two-point conversion pass to Brice Hunter pulled Georgia within two points of the Yellow Jackets. With 7:23 remaining in the contest, the Bulldogs mounted another long drive from their own 10-yard line. Sixteen plays and nearly seven minutes later, the Bulldogs' Kanon Parkman booted an ugly, line-drive kick that cleared the cross bar for a Georgia field goal and an 18–17 lead. Georgia Tech's final drive ended when Davis was sacked by defensive lineman Phillip Daniels and lost a fumble.

Ray Goff received his final victory ride to midfield on the shoulders of seniors Whit Marshall, Paul Taylor, and David Weeks. "If you're going to leave," said Goff, "it's really hard to leave if you lose your last game to your biggest rival." As tears ran down his face after the comeback, upset victory, Goff added, "If I'm going to go out at Georgia, I couldn't go out with a better group." Taylor, a significant member of Goff's last group, declared, "After all the adversity we've been through these past couple of years, today it all came together for Georgia. It all came together for Coach Goff."

It also all came together against the Yellow Jackets for Ward and Kirtsey. Ward, broken wristbone and all, completed 23 of 33 passes for 242 yards. Kirtsey, who missed the entire first quarter, rushed for 99 yards on 26 carries and scored both of Georgia's two touchdowns.

Shortly after the game, Goff joked, "Maybe they'll let me coach until we lose again." In essence, that is exactly what happened— the Bulldogs later received a bid from the Peach Bowl, where they lost to Virginia 34–27 on a last-minute kickoff return for a touchdown by the Cavaliers.

Toward the end of his coaching career at Georgia, Goff once said, "Boy, it's tough to follow a legend," speaking of his succession of Dooley. Goff added that people had asked him, "Who wants to follow a guy with all that success? You don't have a chance!" While Goff's 1991 and 1992 seasons are two of the more successful in Georgia football history, he achieved only three winning campaigns in seven years and found out that it was indeed tough to follow in Dooley's footsteps.

chapter 18

A Satisfactory Five-Year Run

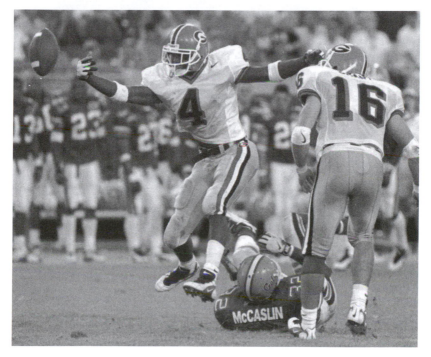

Champ Bailey (No. 4) was a magician with the football and one of the most versatile athletes to ever wear the Red and Black.

Bobo and Edwards Shine in Overtime

Following Ray Goff's departure from Georgia, Jim Donnan was named the Bulldogs' head football coach on Christmas Day of 1995. Donnan had coached six seasons at Marshall, where he compiled a 64–21 record, including capturing a Division I-AA national championship in 1992. Donnan was an All-ACC quarterback at North Carolina State in 1967. Interestingly, in his final college game, he guided the Wolfpack to a 14–7 victory over Georgia in the Liberty Bowl.

The Dogs got off to an abysmal 3–5 start in '96, the program's worst record after eight games since 1961. Making matters worse, three of the five losses—Southern Miss, South Carolina, and Kentucky—were considered upsets at the hands of lesser opponents.

Georgia's main problem was a sputtering offense that was averaging only 16 points and 327 total yards per game. After promising seasons in 1994 and 1995, quarterback Mike Bobo had been a major disappointment, completing only 48 percent of his passes and throwing more than twice as many interceptions as touchdowns (15–7). Georgia's next opponent, Auburn, was ranked 20th in the country and led the conference in takeaways and the nation in interceptions. In addition, the Bulldogs had not defeated a ranked team since the 1993 Citrus Bowl against Ohio State, having a 0–13–1 record against ranked opposition since that season.

It was announced the week of the Auburn game that Mike Bobo had been benched for his season-long struggles. Starting in his place was senior Brian Smith, a career backup who achieved a 3–0 record as Georgia's starting quarterback in 1995. Also not starting was running back Robert Edwards. After moving positions from cornerback, Edwards had also shown tremendous promise in '95, but, during the first eight games of 1996, had been susceptible to fumbling the ball. True freshman Patrick Pass would be starting for Edwards.

In the 100th game between Georgia and Auburn, the Tigers, as expected, held a comfortable 28–7 lead in the second quarter.

The aftermath of the first score of the game, a 21-yard touchdown pass from Dameyune Craig to Robert Baker, is an incident known to almost every Georgia fan. After Baker scored, he sauntered up to Uga V, only to be lunged at by the Georgia mascot and nearly bitten. This is perhaps the most recognized still shot in UGA football history.

The Bulldogs were trailing by three touchdowns with slightly more than six minutes remaining in the second quarter, and their offense needed a major boost. Although quarterback Smith had performed adequately, completing five of six passes for 40 yards, he was benched for former starter Bobo. "I knew we we're going to fight," said Bobo regarding his insertion into the game. "We were down 28–7, so we had nothing to lose." Bobo promptly engineered a Georgia drive that culminated in a two-yard touchdown run by Torin Kirtsey just before halftime.

Early in the final quarter, Bobo connected with Hines Ward for a 67-yard score that pulled Georgia within seven points of Auburn. Late in the game, Bobo brought the Bulldogs 52 yards in eight plays to the Tigers' 30-yard line. On third down and 18, with only one second to play in regulation, Bobo flung a pass toward the front, right corner of the end zone, just beyond the goal line. Sophomore Corey Allen outjumped an Auburn defender and caught an unbelievable touchdown. Hap Hines's extra point tied the score 28–28, and Georgia had forced the first overtime game in SEC football history.

On Georgia's first three possessions of overtime, Edwards scored three touchdowns that were matched by Auburn's scoring of three touchdowns. In the fourth overtime with the score tied 49–49, Kirtsey's one-yard scoring run and Hines's point after gave the Bulldogs a seven-point lead. On the Tigers' possession, three plays netted only seven yards. Facing fourth down and three on the 18-yard line, Craig started to his right on an option but was dragged down by Georgia's Jason Ferguson and Brandon Tolbert short of gaining a first down. In four overtimes, the Bulldogs had defeated the Tigers 56–49.

Against a staunch defense and after struggling all season on the offensive side of the ball, the Bulldogs gained 556 total yards, scored eight touchdowns, and did not commit a single turnover in their victory. Off the bench, Edwards was responsible for 134 rushing and receiving yards, including gaining 98 of Georgia's 100 total yards in the four overtimes. Ward's 175 receiving yards tied for the sixth-most in school history, while Bobo, who did not play in the first quarter and a half, passed for 360 yards on 21 of 37 passes with no interceptions.

Coach Donnan was carried off the field by his players after the memorable victory. It was one of only a few shining moments during a difficult inaugural season at Georgia for the Bulldogs' new coach. The following week, Donnan's Dogs suffered their fourth upset of the season, falling to Ole Miss 31–27 after having a 27–14 third-quarter lead.

Bobo finished his junior season brilliantly, throwing for six touchdowns and only one interception in the final three games. Nevertheless, his best performance was coming off the bench to stimulate a stagnant offense in rallying Georgia over Auburn. "It's the best feeling I've ever had," said Bobo after the game. "The biggest win of my life." An even bigger win for the quarterback occurred nearly a year later in Jacksonville.

Donnan's Drought-Breakers

The difficulties the Bulldogs encountered during a considerable portion of the 1990s included their inability to defeat both Florida and Tennessee. Georgia and its two border rivals are all members of the SEC Eastern Division. Toward the end of the decade and while the Bulldogs' droughts against Florida and Tennessee continued, the question was not whether Georgia could win its division, but whether or not the Bulldogs would finish in third place.

Though Vince Dooley boasted a 17–7–1 career record against Florida, Georgia hadn't defeated the Gators since Goff won his first game against them in 1989. Florida coach Steve Spurrier was a perfect 7–0 against the Bulldogs with a winning margin of more than 26 points, including nearly a 38-point average margin in the three previous meetings (1994 through 1996). For a few years, stories had been told that a cocky Spurrier would often say, "If you go to Georgia, you're never going to beat the Gators."

In 1997, Georgia was experiencing its best season in five years—it had a 6–1 record and was ranked 14th in the nation. National champions in 1996 and seeking their fifth-consecutive conference championship, the Gators were ranked sixth and were 20½-point favorites over the Bulldogs. "We're still underdogs," said Georgia linebacker Greg Bright prior to the game. "We know a lot of people don't give us a chance. But like Coach Donnan tells us, nobody is invincible. Superman is dead."

The Bulldogs held a 14–3 lead at halftime on two touchdown runs by Edwards. In the third quarter, the Gators scored on two rushing touchdowns of their own and had a three-point edge. After Florida's second touchdown, on likely the most important possession of the game, quarterback Bobo promptly drove Georgia 78 yards in 11 plays to Edwards's third touchdown run late in the third quarter. The Bulldogs had regained the momentum and would score two more touchdowns and a field goal in the final quarter to upset the Gators 37–17.

The three-touchdown underdog Bulldogs had defeated Florida by nearly three touchdowns in what remains one of the biggest upsets in Georgia football history. "They outcoached us and outplayed us—the whole bit," said a humble Spurrier in defeat. "We have no excuses. They just beat us. I just don't know what else you can say."

Three seasons later, in 2000, Georgia was experiencing yet another losing streak to a conference rival. The Bulldogs had lost nine consecutive games to Tennessee and had not defeated the Volunteers since 1988, Dooley's final season as coach. At the time, Georgia also had not defeated a ranked team at home since 1991. In 2000, Tennessee entered the game ranked 21st in the nation as a crowd of 86,520 gathered at Sanford Stadium.

The 3–1 and number-19 Bulldogs scored early in the game on a one-yard run by Jasper Sanks. Georgia's defense held Tennessee without a first down for the first 20 minutes. The Volunteers, however, scored 10 consecutive points and had a three-point advantage early in the third quarter. Georgia immediately recaptured the lead 14–10 with 10:08 remaining in the third quarter following a second touchdown run by Sanks.

Late in the third quarter, the Bulldogs began a drive from their own one-yard line. Ten plays and 99 yards later, Musa Smith scored on a one-yard run. Georgia held a comfortable 21–10 advantage it would not relinquish.

With roughly three minutes left in the game, Georgia students and fans began scaling the hedges that surrounded Sanford Stadium's field. With 1:13 remaining, Georgia's Tim Wansley intercepted A.J. Suggs to seemingly clinch the win. Suddenly, despite the presence of security guards and warnings by the announcer, many of the Georgia faithful poured onto the playing surface in celebration. After the fans left the field, the Bulldogs ran two plays and ran out the clock for a Georgia victory.

The main difference in beating Tennessee in 2000 as opposed to the previous nine defeats was the play of Georgia's pass defense. In past seasons, Tennessee quarterbacks Heath Shuler, Peyton Manning, and Tee Martin had spectacular passing performances against the Bulldogs. In 2000, Suggs and Casey Clausen combined to complete 18 of 32 passes for only 136 yards, no touchdowns, and were intercepted twice. In addition, Tennessee reached the Bulldogs' 17-yard line or closer on four occasions in the 2000 meeting, only to score a total of three points.

In winning his 100th career game, the 36th at Georgia, Coach Donnan said after the victory, "I thought we played with poise and confidence tonight, and that was good to see." It was also good to see for the many Bulldogs fans who had waited 12 long years for a win over Tennessee.

When Cows Fly...

Despite a 21–19 loss to Georgia Tech in 1998, Georgia finished the regular season with an 8–3 record and a 19th national ranking. The Bulldogs accepted a bid to the Peach Bowl against number 12 Virginia, which was seeking only its second 10-win season in its history.

Chick-fil-A, the bowl's sponsor, decided to give every one of the Georgia Dome's 72,876 spectators a miniature Chick-fil-A toy cow. The cows cost the sponsor $300,000 and had to be hauled to the dome in four tractor-trailer loads. A plush cow was placed in each seat's cup holder and seemed a generous marketing gift from Chick-fil-A's founder, Truett Cathy. Or, was it?

Following a scoreless first quarter, quarterback Quincy Carter of Georgia threw an interception that led to a Virginia touchdown. Following the score, roughly 1,000 of the Chick-fil-A cows rained down from the dome's seats, having been thrown by fans. Within a five-minute span, Carter threw three interceptions, each leading to a Virginia touchdown, leading to even more cows being thrown onto the field. Toward the end of the first half, Carter, who later said, "I gave them 21 points," had completed only three of 13 passes for 17 yards with three interceptions.

On Georgia's last possession of the opening half, the freshman Carter finally found his rhythm and completed all four of his passes on the drive, including an 11-yard touchdown to split end Tony Small. Despite an emergency announcement from the dome's video board asking for spectators to refrain from throwing objects onto the field, more cows were tossed following Small's scoring reception.

In the third quarter, Georgia tied Virginia 21–21 on a Carter-to-Champ-Bailey pass and a 15-yard run by Olandis Gary. Bailey, playing in what would be his last collegiate game, was considered one of college football's most versatile players in the two-platoon era. Against the Cavaliers, the all-purpose junior participated in 113 plays (60 on defense, 42 on offense, and 11 on special teams). In being selected Georgia's defensive MVP, Bailey broke up a critical pass, had 116 yards on kick returns, rushed for nine yards, and gained 73 yards receiving. Gary, who had played for Coach Donnan at Marshall in the 1994 and 1995 season, finished his career at Georgia with nearly 1,100 rushing yards in only two seasons (1997 through 1998), not including the 110 yards on 19 rushes he gained against Virginia.

After Virginia had regained the lead late in the third quarter, touchdown runs by Gary and Carter gave Georgia a 35–27 advantage with 7:01 remaining. The Cavaliers scored with only 1:34 left on the clock on a 30-yard run by quarterback Aaron Brooks; however, Brooks's pass attempt for two points and a tie was broken up by cornerback Jeff Harris.

After the Cavaliers recovered their own onside kick, Brooks drove Virginia to Georgia's 27-yard line. Three plays netted a loss of four yards, and Cavalier kicker Todd Braverman was called upon for a game-winning field-goal attempt with his team down 35–33. With only 19 seconds remaining in the game, Braverman's 48-yard kick hooked unsuccessfully. Immediately following Braverman's miss, it appeared that any fan who had yet to toss his or her toy cow during the game flung it onto the field.

"We got a quarterback that's special," Donnan said of Carter following the victory, "and he showed that in the second half with the plays he made." Carter, who had been selected SEC Freshman of the Year during the season, struggled for nearly an entire half and faced a seemingly insurmountable 21–0 deficit. However, after his slow start, he completed 15 of 20 passes for 205 yards, two touchdowns, and also rushed for a score.

"My teammates believed in me," said Carter. "[Senior safety] Kirby Smart came over to me and said, 'Stick in there. We believe in you.' That meant all the world to me." On a night when cows flew, a freshman quarterback, facing a 21-point deficit became a leader of a triumphant Georgia team.

Melakalikimaka

A preseason favorite to challenge for the SEC title, Georgia began the 2000 campaign by winning six of its first seven games. Nevertheless, an apparently successful year soon turned sour as the Bulldogs lost to Florida, Auburn, and Georgia Tech in the final four weeks of the regular season. On December 4, more than a week after an embarrassing 27–15 loss to Georgia Tech, Donnan was fired as Georgia's head coach despite a respectable 39–19 record.

Bulldogs players persuaded Georgia administrators to allow Donnan to coach the team against Virginia in the Jeep O'ahu Bowl on Christmas Eve. Although surprised and resentful over his firing, Donnan agreed to coach Georgia for one final game only because of loyalty to his players.

One of Donnan's best decisions for 2000 was hiring defensive coordinator Gary Gibbs. Georgia had ranked dead last in the SEC in defense in '99, allowing 383 yards and 26 points per game. Under Gibbs's supervision, the Bulldogs ranked second in the conference in scoring defense while yielding only 313.5 yards per game.

In front of an announced crowd of only 24,187 at Aloha Stadium in Honolulu, Georgia's imposing defense held the Cavaliers scoreless in the first quarter. The Bulldogs scored on a Billy Bennett field goal, a 40-yard run by Terrence Edwards, and fumble recovery by Kentrell Curry.

By the beginning of the fourth quarter, Virginia had cut Georgia's lead to 24–14. But the Bulldogs defense didn't allow the Cavaliers to score in the final quarter and Georgia scored on a touchdown pass from Cory Phillips to Damien Gary and a four-yard fumble recovery by Cap Burnett.

Injuries to starting quarterback Quincy Carter had forced sophomore Phillips into action in five of the final six games, including the O'ahu Bowl. Phillips responded with 400-yard passing games against Kentucky and Georgia Tech and a 213-yard performance versus Virginia. Sophomore split end Terrence Edwards was named the bowl's Most Valuable Player—he rushed for 97 yards on five carries, caught eight passes for 79 yards, and also took some snaps at quarterback.

The enormous O'ahu Bowl MVP trophy was roughly three-fourths the height of its recipient, Edwards. When asked how he was going to get the trophy on Georgia's charter jet back to Atlanta, Edwards responded, "Carry-on, I guess. It'll make a great Christmas present for my mom."

More than anything, Georgia's players desperately wanted to send the likeable Donnan out a winner. Before the start of the second half, All-American defensive tackle Richard Seymour told his coach he was going to sack the opposing quarterback just for him. True to his word, Seymour registered a sack of Virginia's Bryson Spinner early in the third quarter and in tribute pointed to Donnan on the sideline.

"I feel really happy our players were able to achieve their goals, not that they won it for me," said Donnan following the 37–14 victory. "We won it for Georgia, and we represented Georgia in a first class-manner."

Although Donnan achieved a satisfactory overall record while at Georgia, he was only 6–14 against Tennessee, Florida, Auburn, and Georgia Tech, while winning only seven of 20 against ranked opposition. Nevertheless, he departed as just one of two Bulldogs coaches, along with Dooley, to win eight or more games in four consecutive campaigns. He remains the only Georgia coach to date to record four straight bowl victories.

chapter 19

Richt Returns Bulldogs to Glory

Mark Richt is doused after the Bulldogs beat Arkansas 30–3 in the SEC championship at t Georgia Dome in Atla on December 7, 200

New Hire Thrown into the Fire

On December 21, 2000, Mark Richt, Florida State's offensive coordinator, accepted the head football coaching position at Georgia, although it was not announced until five days later, following the completion of the Bulldogs' 2000 season. The 40-year old Richt and his Dogs began the 2001 campaign by winning two of their first three games, losing to number-21 South Carolina. Despite the early loss, Georgia was receiving favorable reviews in large part because of freshman quarterback David Greene, a redshirt freshman who was impressive in the new coach's offense.

Imagine the seemingly hopeless task Georgia faced in its fourth game of 2001. The Bulldogs, with a newcomer coach and quarterback, had to meet number-six Tennessee in front of nearly 108,000 spectators at Neyland Stadium, regarded as one of the loudest and most intimidating venues in all of collegiate athletics. Under coach Phil Fulmer, the Volunteers were 51–4 at home and had not lost to an unranked team at Neyland Stadium since 1992. Georgia had not won at Knoxville since 1980, losing five consecutive games, and was considered a major underdog in the game. In addition, the Volunteers had college football's best defense against the rush and sought revenge for its loss to Georgia the previous season.

It appeared as if Tennessee would easily coast to a victory as it took an early 14–3 lead on two touchdown passes from Casey Clausen. The turning point of the contest came early in the second quarter when Georgia's Damien Gary returned a punt 72 yards for a score, the Bulldogs' first punt return for a touchdown since 1993. Later in the quarter, Georgia capped a six-play, 56-yard drive with a 15-yard touchdown pass from Greene to freshman Fred Gibson. The Volunteers retaliated with a field goal to tie the score 17–17 before halftime.

Following a scoreless third quarter, Georgia's Billy Benne kicked a 31-yard field goal with 5:44 remaining in the game, a the Bulldogs held a 20–17 advantage. Tennessee began dri for a late score until Jermaine Phillips intercepted Clausen 1:53 left on the clock. At that point, Georgia appeared to finally defeated Tennessee in Knoxville. However, the Bulldogs gained just six yards in three plays and burned only 32 seconds off the clock before they were forced to punt.

With 1:21 remaining from their own 22-yard line, the Volunteers gained 16 yards in their first three plays. From the 38-yard line, Clausen dumped a short pass to tailback Travis Stephens, who took full advantage of great blocking and streaked down his left sideline for a 62-yard score. Only 44 seconds remained in the ballgame as Tennessee led 24–20.

Greene said later of Coach Richt at that moment, "I looked into his eyes and could tell he was confident we could score with 40 seconds left."

A short, squib kickoff by Tennessee was picked up by upback Randy McMichael at Georgia's 34-yard line and returned seven yards. With 42 seconds left, Greene completed a 13-yard pass to Gary, followed by an incomplete pass. Consecutive completions to McMichael of 26 and 14 yards ensued, and Georgia possessed the ball on Tennessee's 6-yard line with 10 seconds remaining.

"P-44-Haynes" was the play call that worked to perfection— Greene found fullback Verron Haynes wide open in the end zone for a six-yard scoring pass. The play will always be one of the most memorable and significant in Georgia football history. The Bulldogs won 26–24 as the remaining five seconds ran out during the following kickoff.

"I give Coach Richt all the credit," said senior Haynes following the game. "I'm kind of mad this is my last year because I would love to have played all four years under him." Of Georgia's 15 seniors in 2001, it is likely that many of them shared the same assessment.

In the first road game of his career in an extremely hostile environment, Greene completed 21 of 34 passes for 303 yards and two touchdowns. Tight end McMichael, responsible for two key ceptions on the game-winning drive, was his primary target, tching a total of six passes for 108 yards.

"We've had a hard time winning big games," said Greene fol-g the win. "They always said we had the potential. We knew re good enough to play with the big teams."

The Richt regime officially began with the extraordinary victory at Neyland Stadium, and it appeared that the Bulldogs possessed an exceptional quarterback to guide them for the next four years. In addition, it looked like Georgia was not only good enough to be competitive with the best but was on the cusp of becoming one of those "big teams."

A Second Chance

At the age of nine, Tony Milton of Tallahassee, Florida, left home to stay with whomever would take him and wherever he could find an available bed. From then on, he had no contact with his father and very little with his mother. Despite the adversity, he starred on his high school football team and was recruited by several major college programs, including Florida State and its offensive coordinator, Mark Richt.

Unfortunately, Milton couldn't meet the necessary entrance test scores and was denied a scholarship from any school. Syracuse, however, was willing to recognize him as a partial qualifier prior to the 1999 football season. Unwilling to leave his girlfriend and newborn son behind in Tallahassee, Milton declined Syracuse's offer.

He found work at a hotel but often was forced to seek shelter and sleep in his car. "Hey, coming from where I come from, that was luxury," said Milton in 2002. "My car had leather seats."

Milton could have chosen a path similar to what some of his friends and two of his brothers had opted for—a path that eventually led to prison. Instead, prior to the 2001 football season, Milton decided to give football a second chance. He approached Richt, who was in his first season as Georgia's head coach, and asked if he could try out for the football team. "[Mark Richt] gave me second chance at life, basically," said Milton. "Playing footbal something I love to do."

Coach Richt asked Milton what position he wanted to "He told me, 'Coach, I don't care what I play,'" said Richt. want a chance to be somebody.'"

In 2001, Milton pulled a hamstring and was redshirted for the season. He began the 2002 campaign as Georgia's number-two tailback behind Musa Smith. In the sixth game of the season, against number-10 Tennessee, sixth-ranked Georgia led 18–13 with 1:43 left in the game. The Bulldogs had the ball on the Volunteers' 35-yard line facing fourth down and two. Milton, who had carried the ball only 19 times all season, was inserted into the game for Smith, who was suffering from an injured neck. On a gutsy call by Richt, Georgia decided to gamble and go for the first down. Quarterback Greene pitched the ball to Milton, who ran around the right end for 25 yards and the critical first down. Georgia ran out the remaining clock and defeated a top-10 team in Sanford Stadium for the first time in 11 years.

Two weeks later, Smith broke his thumb and was forced to miss the Kentucky game. In his place, Milton would be making his first collegiate start. "People always ask me if I'm nervous when I get into games," said Milton prior to the Kentucky game. "After what I've been through, how can I get nervous?"

Milton filled in admirably for Smith, rushing for 78 yards on 18 carries in a 52–24 victory over the Wildcats. In the 14 games of Georgia's SEC championship season of 2002, only one player besides Smith started at tailback for Georgia and led the team in rushing for a single game—Milton. Milton finished the season second on the squad in rushing with 314 yards on 82 carries.

With the emergence of tailbacks Michael Cooper, Kregg Lumpkin, Danny Ware, and Thomas Brown, Milton's playing time steadily decreased over his final three seasons at Georgia (2003–2005). He did make three additional starts at tailback in 2003 and scored his only collegiate touchdown against Kentucky 2004 on a two-yard run late in the game. For his career, he hed for 410 yards and caught 19 passes.

Milton had initially told Coach Richt that he wanted to be ebody." Given a second opportunity in life, he did just that as gia Bulldog.

Greene-to-Johnson Finishes Drill

Prior to coaching his first game at Georgia Richt and his assistants adopted the motto and rallying cry, "finish the drill," with their players. The creed began during preseason mat drills of 2001, continued throughout an admirable 8–4 campaign in Richt's first season, and seemed to have been set in full motion in 2002 as Georgia appeared headed for an SEC championship.

Entering its meeting with number-24 Auburn on November 16, seventh-ranked Georgia had won nine of its 10 games—only a victory over the Tigers stood in the Bulldogs' way of an SEC East title. Georgia's 2002 squad was likely its best since the early 1980s and was in good position to win its first divisional title

David Greene fires a pass over the line against Kentucky on November 6, 2004, in Lexington.

(since the SEC divided into two sections in 1992) and capture its first SEC championship in 20 years. Nevertheless, Georgia had lost three games in a row to Auburn in the South's oldest football rivalry and was only 2–10 for all time in games when both teams were ranked.

Quarterback Greene was looking to help extend Coach Richt's two-year record to 8–0 when playing on an opponent's home field. Greene had visited Auburn's Jordan-Hare Stadium on a recruiting trip during the spring of 1999. Greene's father, grand-father, and sister had attended Auburn, and he had considered fol-lowing in their footsteps to become a Tiger. However, Greene and his father were unable to arrange a meeting with any of the coaches. The Auburn assistants did not seem to have much inter-est in recruiting Greene, an inconsideration that turned out to be a critical mistake.

Minus standout receivers Terrence Edwards and Gary because of injuries, Greene and the rest of Georgia's offense could only muster 63 total yards by halftime as Auburn led 14–3. The Bulldogs' deficit could have easily been greater, but safety Sean Jones intercepted two Tigers passes and recovered a fumble all in the first quarter.

To begin the second half, Georgia drove 67 yards in 10 plays with Greene scoring on a one-yard plunge. Auburn retaliated with a touchdown, but the Bulldogs came right back down the field for their second touchdown in two third-quarter possessions. Greene fumbled into the end zone, where offensive tackle Jon Stinchcomb, who had made a moving, motivational halftime speech, fell on the ball for a score. Bennett's extra point was suc-cessful, and Georgia trailed 21–17 late in the third quarter.

Auburn's next six possessions each lasted only three plays and resulted in punts. Following the sixth kick, Georgia had the all on its own 41-yard line with 1:58 remaining in the game. A pass from Greene to Gibson to the Tigers' 14-yard line soon ved. After three incompletions and a five-yard penalty, ia, behind by four points with 1:31 remaining in the game, urth down and 15 on the 19-yard line.

The play came in from the sideline, "70-X-Takeoff." Split end Michael Johnson's number had been called. Johnson, a backup all season, had been inserted into the starting position because of Edwards's shoulder injury. "I didn't want to let [the] Bulldog Nation down," Johnson said.

Greene dropped back to pass and pump-faked to his right toward Gibson, who was acting as a decoy. Greene then lofted a pass in the back left corner of the end zone. There, Johnson jumped up over an Auburn defensive back and caught the ball while pulling it away from the defender for a phenomenal touchdown.

"It was a beautiful ball," said Johnson of the game-winning pass thrown to him. "It was like I was in a daze."

Most everyone was in a daze and amazed that Georgia had completed a fourth-down miracle to assume its first lead of the game. Auburn had one more opportunity but turned the ball over on downs before it could get within field-goal range. The 24–21 Georgia victory sealed the Bulldogs' first SEC East divisional title and had many players to credit in finishing the drill against Auburn.

Jones, besides his three takeaways, recorded 11 tackles and also returned four punts for 75 yards. Michael Johnson had only caught 11 passes all season in a backup role, however against Auburn, he had 13 receptions for 141 yards, including one of the greatest catches in Georgia football history. In addition, Greene passed for 232 yards, was responsible for two touchdowns, and once again proved that he could win on the road, regardless of crowd hostility.

"This is the best thing I've ever been through in football," said Greene following Georgia's fifth win of the season by six points or less. In 2002, he and the rest of the Bulldogs would experience even better things, namely, Georgia's first SEC title since 1982 following a 30–3 victory over Arkansas in the SEC championship game and a 26–13 win in the Sugar Bowl versus Florida State. Georgia finished the season with a 13–1 record and a numb— three national ranking. This was the most wins in school histor— a single season and the Bulldogs' highest final ranking sinc— 1980 national championship.

The Davids' Last Stand

After an 11–3 record and a number-seven ranking for Georgia in 2003, there were high expectations for the Bulldogs the following season. Georgia was ranked third and fourth in the Associated Press and Coaches polls for 2004. In fact, many believed the Bulldogs would contend for the national championship. So, there was some disappointment when Georgia was 8–2 and ranked eighth entering its regular-season finale versus Georgia Tech. There would be no national championship in 2004 and, for the first time in three years, no chance for an SEC title. However, the championship of the state of Georgia was at stake.

The Georgia Tech contest would be the last game for 14 senior Bulldogs at Sanford Stadium. The members of the 2004–2005 class had been freshmen when Richt arrived and had achieved an impressive 40–10 record in their four seasons. This class also featured Greene, one of the best quarterbacks ever at Georgia, and David Pollack, the most decorated defensive player of all time at the school.

"This will be the last Dog Walk, the last time putting on the Red and Black and coming out of our locker room," said Pollack a day prior to the Georgia Tech game. "There are so many memories at Sanford Stadium...there's nothing like playing at home."

Four weeks earlier, Pollack had become Georgia's all-time career leader in sacks. The defensive end had also been named first-team All-American for the third time—only the second player in Georgia football history, besides Herschel Walker, to be selected first-team All-American in three seasons. Pollack would eventually receive the Lombardi Award for the nation's most outstanding lineman, the Chuck Bednarik Award for the defensive player of the year, the Ted Hendricks Award for the second time as the top defensive end in the country, and selected SEC Defensive Player of the Year by the coaches and media.

On an extremely cold and wet day in Athens, Greene threw a ...ard touchdown pass to Gibson early against Georgia Tech. In ...cond quarter, D.J. Shockley filled in for Greene, who had ... his thumb. Andy Bailey kicked a field goal, then Shockley passed to Reggie Brown for a score as the Bulldogs led comfortably at halftime 16-0.

In the third quarter and with tens of thousands of spectators having left the stadium because of the weather, Shockley and the offense could not move the football, netting negative yardage for the quarter. On the other hand, Georgia Tech, in the third quarter, began four possessions at Georgia's 43-yard line, the 14, the 38, and at midfield. The end result of the favorable field position was 13 points scored by Georgia Tech as the Dogs' comfortable lead disappeared.

David Greene was inserted midway through the fourth quarter to revive the Bulldogs' struggling offense. Fighting through pain, the senior quarterback instantly led Georgia on a 10-play, 40-yard drive resulting in a 44-yard field goal by freshman Brandon Coutu, the first of his career.

David Pollack (No. 47) was a fiery leader and the most decorated defensive players in Georgia Bull history.

Down 19–13, Georgia Tech began its last drive. Quarterback Reggie Ball completed a 38-yard pass to Georgia's 21-yard line with 1:32 remaining in the game. The pressure was on Georgia's defense to hold Georgia Tech but, according to Pollack, "To tell you the truth, we kind of like it when the pressure is on us."

As the Yellow Jackets threatened, the Bulldogs' defense—led all season and throughout their collegiate careers by linebacker Odell Thurman, safety Thomas Davis, sophomore defensive end Quentin Moses, and most notably, Pollack—kept Georgia Tech from reaching the goal line.

Ball completed a screen pass for no gain on first down. On second down, he was sacked by Moses for an 11-yard loss. It was Moses's third sack of the game, while Pollack had recorded two sacks earlier in the contest. Ball spiked the ball on third down to stop the clock, and Georgia Tech faced fourth down and 21 on Georgia's 32-yard line.

On the next play, Ball rolled out to his right while being chased by Pollack and inexplicably threw the ball out of bounds. Georgia Tech had turned the ball over on downs, and the Bulldogs won the game 19–13. Apparently, Ball had become "discombobulated," according to his head coach, Chan Gailey. The Yellow Jackets' quarterback had lost track of the downs and believed the scoreboard indicated it was third down when it was actually his final opportunity.

Georgia would win its final game of the 2004 season against Wisconsin in the Outback Bowl. Greene threw for 264 yards and two touchdowns in the 24–21 victory, while Pollack recorded four tackles and three sacks on his way to becoming the bowl's Most Valuable Player. It was the last game for seniors David Greene and David Pollack, two of the finest Bulldogs to ever to don the Red and Black.

chapter 20

The Latest Edition

Mikey Henderson holds on to the ball for a touchdown as he's pulled down by Western Kentucky's Tanner Siewart during an eventful game on September 2, 2006.

Mikey's Redemption

In 2005, Georgia earned a trip to the SEC championship game for the third time in four years and, for the second season since 2002, won the SEC title and received a Sugar Bowl bid. Entering 2006, the Bulldogs had lost 15 of 26 starters (including specialists) from Georgia's 10–3 campaign in '05. Despite the losses of consensus All-Americans Greg Blue and Max Jean-Giles, and four additional first-team All-SEC selections, including quarterback D.J. Shockley, the Bulldogs began the 2006 season ranked 15th and 14th, respectively, in the Associated Press and Coaches preseason polls.

Georgia opened its season against Western Kentucky before a sellout crowd of 92,746 at Sanford Stadium. With no score and 10:44 remaining in the opening quarter, junior Mikey Henderson entered the game for Georgia to receive a Hilltopper punt. Henderson, who had played very little during his first two seasons as a Bulldog, was only returning punts because Thomas Flowers was serving a suspension. After only two seasons at Georgia, Flowers ranked eighth of all time at the school in career punt-return yardage, averaging an impressive 14.2 yards per return.

Henderson received Western Kentucky's kick on his own 34-yard line and, on his first collegiate return, broke free and was heading for an apparent 66-yard touchdown. As Henderson neared the goal line, he one-handedly raised the football in what turned out to be a premature celebration. Near the 2-yard line, the ball fell out of his hand. When the dismayed returner regained possession of the football, Henderson was standing on the end line and the ball was awarded to Western Kentucky. The replay booth reviewed the play, but to Georgia's disappointment, it was ruled that the decision on the field stood, and the Hilltoppers were given possession on a touchback.

From its 20-yard line, Western Kentucky ran three plays for only one yard and was forced to punt. Coach Mark Richt was reluctant to insert Henderson to return the second punt, not because of his earlier mistake but because of an injured hamstring. "But he begged me to go back in, so I let him," said Richt

Perhaps the only suitable aftermath following Henderson's blunder and the one result that could lessen any embarrassment and discomfort would be to return the next punt for a score. The stage was set, and a possible opportunity was created for this to happen. With 9:28 left in the quarter and just over a minute after his initial return, Henderson miraculously returned the second punt for a 67-yard touchdown. "That's the only thing I could think about," said Henderson on securing the football on his second return. "I was holding that ball so tight, nobody could have taken it away from me."

Georgia went on to conquer the Hilltoppers 48–12. Quarterbacks Joe Tereshinski and true freshman Matthew Stafford each passed for touchdowns, while backs Danny Ware, Thomas Brown, and Kregg Lumpkin each rushed for scores. The Bulldogs' defense limited Western Kentucky to only 193 total yards and just 1.9 yards per rushing attempt.

For the 2006 college football season, several rule changes were implemented to shorten games, including starting the clock after changes of possession as soon as the ball is spotted instead of when the ball is snapped. Because of the rule changes, Georgia ran only 52 offensive plays for 295 yards.

Against Tennessee five weeks later, Henderson returned a punt 86 yards for his second touchdown of the season. Henderson finished the year ranked fifth in the nation, with a punt-return average of 14.7 yards, and more than made up for his debut punt return.

Richt's Junkyard Dogs

Erk Russell is undoubtedly the most distinguished and highly esteemed assistant coach in the history of Georgia football. The Bulldogs' defensive coordinator from 1964 to 1980, Russell was known for his bald—at times bleeding—head, which he would often slam against the chests of players' shoulder pads during pregame warmups for motivational purposes. Most importantly, he coached defenses that did not always have the best talent but was able to mold his players into determined, overachieving defenders.

Chris Welton, Georgia's starting roverback in 1980, said he gladly worked hard for Coach Russell "because you know he's working hard," Welton once said. "You know nobody is gonna be working harder than he does."

At Georgia, Russell had the following motto on his office's bulletin board: "If life deals you lemons, turn it into lemonade." Russell was handed lemons prior to the 1975 season—a group of small, undistinguished, and inexperienced defensive players. He turned those players into one of college football's best defenses—the Junkyard Dogs.

Russell left Georgia following the national championship season of 1980 to win three national championships as head coach at Georgia Southern. He retired after eight seasons as the Eagles' coach, compiling an 83–22–1 record from 1982 to 1989.

On September 8, 2006, Russell died at the age of 80 from an apparent stroke. In honor of his memory, Georgia players wore black "ERK" emblems on the backs of their helmets for their game the following day against South Carolina in Columbia. South Carolina head coach Steve Spurrier, considered an offensive genius, consistently had tremendous success against Georgia during his 16 years as a college football coach, winning 11 of 13 games against the Bulldogs while averaging nearly 35 points per game.

Following a Brandon Coutu field goal in the first quarter, Georgia extended its lead to 10–0 in the second quarter on a Danny Ware touchdown run. In the same quarter, defensive end Charles Johnson tackled South Carolina's Mike Davis in the end zone for a safety. Johnson also recorded five tackles for the game, four of which were for losses. Coutu would add another field goal before halftime and one in the final quarter as the Bulldogs shut out the Gamecocks 18–0.

South Carolina's reputable offense was held to 255 yards, its lowest output of the season. During the contest, the Gamecocks had the ball on Georgia's 1-yard line, the 2-yard line, and inside the Bulldogs' 20-yard line on another possession but could not score any points against Georgia's defense. It was the first time a

Spurrier-coached college team had been shut out in 193 games, dating back to 1987 when he coached at Duke. It was also the first time the Bulldogs had shut out an SEC opponent on the road since Kentucky in 1980—Russell's last season at Georgia.

"One of the things we talked about was trying to honor Coach Russell, and the best way to do that was to play like Junkyard Dogs," said Richt following the game. "And that's what our guys did."

True to the form of Russell's Georgia defenses of the past, the Bulldogs bent and allowed South Carolina several scoring opportunities but never broke against the Gamecocks. "You get the ball that close [to Georgia's goal line], it's supposed to be easy," said Georgia linebacker Danny Verdun Wheeler of the Gamecock offense, "but not against the Junkyard Dogs."

Ralphie Runs, Joe Relieves

In the summer prior to the 2006 season, the University of Georgia invited Colorado University to bring its mascot when the two schools played football on September 23 in Athens. Coupled with Georgia's Uga VI, the arrival of Colorado's Ralphie IV, a 900-pound, female buffalo, would bring together perhaps college football's two best-known mascots.

Nine-year old Ralphie IV was born on a ranch in Montana owned by CNN's founder and Atlanta billionaire Ted Turner. Colorado's Ralphies rarely made trips to regular-season road games, and the trek to Athens would be the first in 25 years. Three days before the game, Ralphie IV departed for Athens on a 1,500-mile journey in her 20-foot, black-and-gold trailer. Along for the ride was a camera from ESPN's *GameDay* preview show to chronicle her excursion.

Prior to the game, Ralphie was quite popular at Sanford Stadium, and many Georgia fans posed with the buffalo for photographs. "I wish we got this kind of reception in Boulder," said one of Ralphie's handlers. "It's been a great experience. We've been greeted with open arms. Southern hospitality at its finest."

Prior to kickoff for 30 seconds, Sanford Stadium witnessed one of the most unique sights in all of collegiate athletics. Accompanied by nine handlers, Ralphie led Colorado onto the field, rounded the end zone, and ran directly back toward the corner of the stadium where he started. Most individuals expected this to be the highlight of the day for Colorado—the Bulldogs were nearly four-touchdown favorites over the winless Buffaloes.

In the fourth quarter, Colorado led 13–0 on two field goals by Mason Crosby and a one-yard touchdown run by quarterback Bernard Jackson. Colorado head coach Dan Hawkins, who had coached Boise State in a loss to Georgia the season before, and his Buffaloes appeared to be on their way to handing the Bulldogs one of the biggest upsets in their history.

Freshman Joe Cox had relieved quarterback Matthew Stafford for Georgia late in the third quarter to energize a sluggish offense. On the Bulldogs' second drive during the final quarter, Cox threw a screen pass to fullback Brannan Southerland on second down and 9 from Colorado's 23-yard line. Southerland caught the screen and rumbled for a Georgia touchdown, with 9:11 remaining in the game.

On their next drive, the Bulldogs drove to the Buffaloes' 12-yard line but turned the ball over on downs. Georgia's defense, however, forced Colorado to run three plays and punt, giving the ball back to the Dogs with 2:29 left in the contest.

Three Cox completions and a Lumpkin run netted 23 yards and gave Georgia the ball on Colorado's 20-yard line. Facing third down and 5 with under a minute remaining on the clock, Cox threw a perfect pass to tight end Martrez Milner for a touchdown. Coutu's point after gave Georgia a 14–13 lead.

Tony Taylor of Georgia intercepted Jackson at the 50-yard line on the game's final drive, and Georgia squeaked out a one-point victory. For the game, Lumpkin rushed for 52 of the Bulldogs' 54 net rushing yards. Heroic Cox completed 10 of 13 passes for 154 yards and two touchdowns and, in relief, saved Georgia from what would have been a devastating loss.

Following the game, Cox indicated it was a "dream scenario" that he orchestrated the Bulldogs' victory and said, "I was pretty surprised when they made the switch [for Cox to relieve at quarterback]…I was ready for this situation and it worked out well."

Cox's fine performance against Colorado earned him his only start of the 2006 season the following week at Ole Miss. The number 10–ranked Bulldogs improved their record to 5–0 but once again barely escaped with a 14–9 win.

A Triumphant Turnaround

Ten weeks into the 2006 season, Georgia was enduring its worst year since the 5–6 losing campaign of 1996. After a promising 5–0 start, during which Georgia climbed as high as ninth in the national rankings, the Bulldogs fell completely apart.

The Dogs led Tennessee 24–7 late in the second quarter only to allow the Volunteers to outscore them 44–9 the rest of the contest. A loss to Vanderbilt followed when the Commodores kicked a last-minute field goal for a two-point win.

Matthew Stafford was named MVP in the Bulldogs' remarkable second-half comeback against Virginia Tech in the Chick-fil-A Bowl on December 30, 2006.

After a victory over lowly Mississippi State, the Bulldogs did keep it close in a 21–14 loss to Florida—the eventual national champion. Georgia, a seven-point favorite, lost the fourth of five games to Kentucky on a late touchdown. For the first time in 33 years, the Bulldogs had lost to both Vanderbilt and Kentucky in the same season.

With games remaining against Auburn, Georgia Tech, and perhaps a bowl game, a 6–7 final record for Georgia and its first losing season in 10 years was a possibility. The Bulldogs' consecutive streak of seasons with eight or more wins since 1997 was in serious jeopardy, and the possibility of finishing in the AP's final rankings for the 10th-straight season was highly unlikely. Georgia football had fallen to its lowest point during the six seasons under Richt. Considering the competition they would face in their final games, even the most optimistic fan had little hope Georgia would end the season on a positive note.

Fifth-ranked Auburn, with home-field advantage, had defeated Florida for its only loss of the season and was 11½-point favorites to drop the Bulldogs' record to 6–5. However, Georgia jumped ahead 24–0 in the second quarter and eventually whipped the Tigers 37–15 for the school's 700th all-time football victory.

Freshman quarterback Stafford was brilliant, throwing for 219 yards on 14 of 20 passing. He also rushed for 83 yards, the highest mark during the season for someone other than Lumpkin. For only the second time in 2006, Georgia had a player rush for 100 yards or more as Lumpkin's 105 yards on 21 carries and a touchdown paced the Bulldogs' ground attack. Georgia's defense held Auburn to only 171 total yards, its lowest amount for the season. Roverback Tra Battle tied a school record with three interceptions during the first half, one of which was returned for a score in the second quarter. The 22-point victory was one of the bigger upsets by Georgia in more than 30 years.

Two weeks later the Bulldogs met rival Georgia Tech at Sanford Stadium. The Yellow Jackets were seemingly in the midst of one of their best seasons in decades. They were ranked 16th nationally and had already clinched a spot in the ACC championship game scheduled for the following week. In addition, a ranked Georgia Tech team was 9–0 all-time when playing an unranked Georgia team.

Late in the third quarter, with Georgia Tech leading 3–0, Tony Taylor of Georgia picked up a fumble and raced 29 yards for the game's first touchdown. With the Yellow Jackets later leading 12–7, the Bulldogs began a drive from their own 36-yard line with 8:50 remaining in the game. Georgia drove 64 yards in 12 plays, including seven rushes by tailback Danny Ware and three receptions by Mohamed Massaquoi. With 1:45 left in the game, Stafford completed a four-yard touchdown pass to Massaquoi, and the pair hooked up again for the two-point conversion. On Georgia Tech's last-ditch drive, cornerback Paul Oliver intercepted Tech's Reggie Ball to preserve a 15–12 Georgia victory, the Bulldogs' sixth-consecutive win over their intrastate rival. What many thought was impossible, the Georgia Bulldogs had accomplished in defeating both Auburn and Georgia Tech.

An invitation was extended to Georgia to play Virginia Tech in the Chick-fil-A Bowl. The Bulldogs were considered an underdog, and for two quarters it appeared the pundits were correct. Georgia, performing similar to how it had played in the middle of the season, trailed 21–3 at halftime to 14th-ranked Hokies. Toward the end of the second quarter, and as Georgia left the field for halftime, a scattering of boos from Bulldogs fans could be heard throughout the Georgia Dome. An 18-point deficit to Virginia Tech seemed insurmountable—the Hokies had college football's best scoring defense, total defense, and passing defense and had surrendered only five second-half touchdowns during the entire season.

What Georgia achieved in the second half against Virginia Tech was absolutely remarkable. After punting on their first offensive drive, Georgia's next five possessions ended in three touchdowns and two field goals. The Bulldogs' 28 second-half points all came in a span of only 13:40, while four of Georgia's five scores were set up with an onside kick, two interceptions, and a fumble recovery.

The 18-point comeback by Georgia en route to a 31–24 win was the third-largest deficit in a victory by the Bulldogs in the modern era. Georgia's Stafford was named the Chick-fil-A Bowl's offensive MVP, throwing for 129 yards and a touchdown. Although the Bulldogs only generated 200 total yards, Georgia's defense was stellar, allowing just 189 yards.

A tearful Ray Gant, one of Georgia's starting defensive tackles, was one of many elated Bulldogs following the victory. "It's amazing," said Gant. "I couldn't have dreamt it up any better.... That's Georgia, we never give up. We will never give up."

To their credit, after losing four of five games in 2006, the Bulldogs never gave up when many teams in similar circumstances would have folded. Instead, Georgia responded by consecutively defeating three ranked teams when the Dogs were unranked themselves—all while being an underdog against two of the three opponents. In addition, by the end of the year, the Bulldogs had continued their streak of 10 consecutive seasons of ranking in the AP's final poll, finishing 23rd.

"It's amazing what our guys have done," said Richt following the Chick-fil-A Bowl win. "To change that momentum was monumental. It's a tribute to our leaders, our seniors."

Despite the Bulldogs' four losses in 2006, the season was characterized by what could be argued as Richt's best coaching effort in his six successful campaigns at Georgia. If it is true that the best predictor of future behavior is past behavior, the Georgia Bulldog Nation can be nothing but optimistic regarding the future of the Georgia football program. Under Coach Richt and the accomplished assistants that he surrounds himself with, Georgia football appears destined to continue as one of the most successful programs in the nation.

sources

Augusta Chronicle (1996–2006).

Athens Banner-Herald (1894–2006).

Atlanta Constitution (1892–2006).

Atlanta Journal (1907–2006).

Atlanta Journal Magazine, November 20, 1949.

Bolton, Clyde. *Silver Britches: Inside University of Georgia Football*. West Point, NY: Leisure Press, 1982.

Boyles, Bob, and Paul Guido. *Fifty Years of College Football: A Modern History of America's Most Colorful Sport*. Wilmington, Delaware: Sideline Communications, Inc., 2005.

Cromartie, Bill. *Clean Old-Fashioned Hate*. Nashville, Tennessee: Rutledge Hill Press, 1987.

Cromartie, Bill. *There Goes Herschel*. New York: Leisure Press, 1983.

Ernsberger, Richard. *Bragging Rights: A Season Inside the SEC, College Football's Toughest Conference*. New York: M. Evans and Company, Inc., 2000.

"George Poschner." Wikipedia.com 2006. en.wikipedia.org/wiki/George_Poschner (January 16, 2007).

"Georgia." Jim and Sherri Howell's Home Page. 2006. www.jhowell.net/cf/scores/Georgia.htm (November 29, 2006).

"Georgia Bulldogs." College Football Data Warehouse. 2006. www.cfbdatawarehouse.com/data/div_ia/sec/georgia/index.php (January 20, 2007).

Georgia Institute of Technology Football Media Guide, 2004.

Hannon, Shane. "Charley Trippi." *Online Athens.* 2002. www.onlineathens.com/dogbytes/legends/trippi_02.shtml (December 6, 2006).

Harvard University Football Media Guide, 2004.

MacCambridge, Michael, ed. *ESPN College Football Encyclopedia: The Complete History of the Game.* New York: ESPN Books, 2005.

Macon News, November 29, 1907.

Macon Telegraph (1904–2006).

Martin, Charles E. *I've Seen 'Em All*. Athens, Georgia: The McGregor Company, 1961.

Munson's Greatest Calls: The Greatest Plays in Georgia Football History (video). Atlanta: Cutting Edge Video, 1995.

Official 2006 NCAA Divisions I-A and I-AA Football Records Book. Indianapolis, Indiana: The National Collegiate Athletic Association, 2006.

Outlar, Jesse. *Between the Hedges: A Story of Georgia Football*. Huntsville, Alabama: Strode Publishing, 1973.

Smith, Loran. *Between the Hedges: 100 Years of Georgia Football*. Marietta, Georgia: Longstreet Press, Inc., 1992.

Prugh, Jeff. *Herschel Walker Story*. New York: Ballantine Books, 1983.

Stegeman, John F. *The Ghosts of Herty Field: Early Days on a Southern Gridiron*. Athens, Georgia: University of Georgia Press, 1997.

Sullivan, Buddy. *Hunker Down!: The Story of Dooley's 'Dogs*. LaGrange, Georgia: Stephens Printing Co., 1981.

"Tar Heels Credited with Throwing First Forward Pass." *Tar Heel Times*. 2006. www.tarheeltimes.com/2006/08/tar_heels_credi.html (December 5, 2006).

Thilenius, Ed, and Jim Koger. *No Ifs, No ands, a Lot of Butts: 21 Years of Georgia Football*. Atlanta: Foote & Davies, Inc., 1960.

Troy, Jack. *Leading a Bulldog's Life*. Atlanta: Albert Love, 1948.

University of Georgia Football Media Guide, 1948–2006.

University of Notre Dame Football Media Guide, 2003.

Vanderbilt University Football Media Guide, 2006.

Wilder, Robert E. *Gridiron Glory Days: Football at Mercer, 1892–1942*. Macon, Georgia: Mercer University Press, 1982.